Bluffer's®

GUIDE TO
OPERA

KEITH HANN

© Haynes Publishing 2018
Published June 2018

A CIP Catalogue record for this book
is available from the British Library.

ISBN: 978 1 78521 245 1

Library of Congress control no. 2018932892

Published by Haynes Publishing,
Sparkford, Yeovil, Somerset BA22 7JJ
Tel: 01963 440635
Int. tel: +44 1963 440635
Website: www.haynes.com

Printed in Malaysia.

Series Editor: David Allsop.
Front cover illustration by Alan Capel.

CONTENTS

Pre-performance Prep   5

Tuning Up   7

Opera Choice   15

House Etiquette   33

The Curtain Rises: How Opera Started   39

The Big Aria: The Great Opera Composers   49

Supporting Chorus: The Also-Rans   59

Recitative: Classic Opera Plots and Tunes   77

Long Interval: Opera Supporting Cast   87

Golden Vocal Cords: Great Opera Performers   95

Finale: Operetta, The Musical and Opera Today   103

Curtain Call: A Useful Glossary   113

You will certainly raise eyebrows at Glyndebourne if you offer to keep an eye on the picnic while everyone else troops off to see the show.

PRE-PERFORMANCE PREP

For some people, opera is a religion. Others think it is considerably more important than that. This makes it a field in which the bluffer must tread with particular delicacy to avoid causing offence, or being exposed as the only sane person in the asylum. The object of this short guide is to impart sufficient knowledge to allow the average reader to pass for someone who 'knows a bit about opera' should the need or urge arise.

WHY DO YOU NEED TO KNOW ABOUT OPERA?

A fair question. Perhaps because you risk joining those black-tied punters regularly encountered at grand opera houses, whose body language (fidgeting, sighing and repeated consultations of wristwatches) makes it clear that they would rather be undergoing waterboarding.

They might have found themselves in this unfortunate predicament because opera has become an arm of the 'corporate hospitality' industry, along with every major sporting event. And, while it is apparently true that those with no interest in tennis can pass a perfectly pleasant day at Wimbledon without ever leaving the hospitality suite, you will certainly raise eyebrows at Glyndebourne if you offer to keep an eye on the picnic while everyone else troops off to see the show.

Clearly, those who invite their valued contacts to a night at the opera do so in the belief that they are offering them a treat, not a torture. If, after reading this book, you still feel that opera has nothing to offer, then it will probably be best to try saying a polite 'no' when your next invitation comes along. Either that or prepare yourself by borrowing some exceptionally boring DVDs (steam trains, trolleybuses or boxed sets of *Big Brother* should all do nicely) and practise for your next visit to the opera house by watching them sitting completely still, in perfect silence.

Should you find yourself unable to avoid such an invitation, don't despair. This short but definitive guide will conduct you through the main danger zones encountered in opera discussions and equip you with a vocabulary and an evasive technique that will minimise the risk of being rumbled as a bluffer. It will give you a few easy-to-learn hints and methods that might even allow you to be accepted as an opera lover of rare passion and experience. But it will do more. It will give you the tools to impress legions of marvelling listeners with your knowledge and insight – without anyone discovering that before reading it you didn't know the difference between an Austin Allegro and an *allegro con brio*.

TUNING UP

So let's suppose you're committed to a night at the opera and, for reasons known to anyone who has ever bluffed about anything (that would be all of us), you feel the need to pretend to know more than you do. Here are the answers to some fundamental questions which might help to point you in the right direction.

WHY SHOULD YOU LIKE OPERA?

Where to start? It contains some of the greatest and most memorable music ever written, performed by singers and players of truly staggering virtuosity. Just look at that small woman on the stage (for the traditional fat lady has largely passed into history) and reflect that she is filling the large theatre in which you are sitting with the simple power of her own voice, unaided by amplification. That fact still stuns some cynics after many decades of regular opera-going.

The downside is that it is extremely hard for anyone to perform this trick two nights in a row without doing permanent damage to their vocal cords, so to the intrinsically high cost of opera (large casts, big orchestras, complex sets) is added the further burden of having to dismantle the whole thing each day and install a completely different production for the following night.

WHY DO THEY BOTHER?

Put simply, opera is one of the highest pinnacles of human civilisation. Questioning its worth is a bit like asking why St Peter's, Hagia Sophia or Angkor Wat were built. You are entitled to prefer a night in with *Coronation Street* to a night out at *The Marriage of Figaro*, but the first premise of successful bluffing about opera must be to accept that it is a stunning achievement. Taking the opposite view is the first step on the road that leads to smashing stained-glass windows, defacing icons or directing artillery at 1,500-year-old giant Buddhas.

These religious parallels are not coincidental. Opera mirrors the church in deploying great music and performers to underline its message and draw in believers, and it occupies some of the grandest unconsecrated spaces on the planet. Indeed, it has been remarked that the main difference between an operatic performance and a sung mass is that the opera's collection is taken beforehand – and what a collection it tends to be! If only the church could raise its sights so high, every parish priest in Britain could be housed in the splendour of his or her own Vatican – or massively increase the church's support for the deserving poor, according to taste.

On the other hand, opera delivers no sermons (beyond initial warnings about the use of mobile phones, cameras and recording equipment). It imposes no obligation to exchange an embarrassed handshake with other members of the congregation, or share a plastic cup of instant coffee with them after the performance. And it also positively encourages the expression of emotion at its close in the form of a hearty round of applause (accompanied, if appropriate, by the stamping of feet and the hurling of floral tributes). One rarely enjoys these pleasures in church, even at the louchest of funerals, making opera well worth the additional cost of admission. And, as if it needed to be pointed out, church services generally don't have intermissions with easy access to a bar.

WHERE ARE ITS ROOTS?

Opera not only resembles a religious service, but it is also rooted in the Christian church's desire to reach out to the public and engage them with its message. Pedants may claim that opera's roots go back as far as ancient Greece, with the singing or chanting by the chorus in classical drama. We know with some certainty, though, that 1,000 years ago Western Europe developed a tradition of liturgical plays that included musical components to increase their appeal. No surprise there: just consider the preponderance of musicals in the West End or on Broadway today. Adding music to a 'straight' play clearly increases its pulling power exponentially. Anyone who contends that they 'hate opera but love musicals' has not understood the transference from one to the other, or the hazy and porous dividing line between the two. Enlightenment on this point will follow a bit later.

BUT WHY DO THEY NEED TO SING?

The story of any opera could be enacted without anyone singing or playing a note, just as the plot of a ballet could be conveyed without a lot of people dressing up in tights and tutus and hopping around on blood-drenched tippy-toes. But if you are of a mind to object on these grounds, you are missing the point.

If you have chosen the performance wisely and fail to enjoy yourself, you are either tone deaf or an irredeemable Philistine.

A good opera, performed well, can and should capture all the audience's senses and allow them, for three hours or so (five or more in the case of Wagner), to dismiss their everyday cares completely from their minds. It can successfully mix elation at the quality of the performance with genuine sorrow at the turn of events on stage. Even strong men are often seen furtively reaching for a handkerchief at the end of *Madama Butterfly*. Truly, no one has yet devised a better balm for the soul. Which is why even the most committed sceptic should be prepared to cast aside his or her prejudices and give it a try – preferably through total immersion rather than with one hand still clinging grimly to the side of the pool. Ignore the quirks (though this book will explain some of them) and accept the form as it is. If you have chosen the performance wisely and fail to enjoy yourself, you are either tone deaf or an irredeemable Philistine.

DO YOU NEED TO LEARN A FOREIGN LANGUAGE TO APPRECIATE OPERA?

No, you don't. However, the origins of opera are Italian, so that is the language in which its technical terms are couched and in which the majority of operas are performed. It will greatly increase your chances of being mistaken for an expert if you can absorb a handful of these key terms into your everyday vocabulary.

For example, the words of the opera are contained in a *libretto* (little book), the big number is an *aria* (air), the lady singing it is probably a *soprano* (higher voice), and if she adds some ornamental flourishes they are most likely *coloratura* (colouring) rather than an early sign of dementia (*see* 'Glossary', page 113). If you subsequently run into the man you have seen waving a stick in the orchestra pit (and he is often to be found in the nearest pub after the performance, along with at least half his players, including the entire brass section), he will appreciate being addressed as *maestro* (master), though not half as much as he will enjoy that being prefaced with the emphatically non-Italian phrase: 'What can I get you?'

From the dawn of opera until almost the end of the twentieth century, it was essential to buy a programme and spend a frantic 10 minutes before the performance mugging up on the synopsis in order to have the faintest clue as to what was about to happen on stage. This allowed the dedicated bluffer to gain an important tactical advantage by laughing knowingly at the delivery of certain key lines, confident that 99% of the audience would not have a clue whether or not they were supposed to be funny. Modest bets could be placed with oneself as to how many fellow patrons might be bluffed into joining in.

Sadly, this potential source of amusement has been destroyed by the advent of almost universal surtitles, which provide a simultaneous (if sometimes approximate) translation of the words being uttered on stage. The best the bluffer can manage now is to express contempt for the *sopratitoli* (which, of course, you will know is the Italian for surtitles) on taking his or her seat, and look pointedly at the stage rather than the little screen above it (which is actually pretty good general advice for all members of the audience).

If moved by a particularly fine or affecting performance of an aria, one may be moved to shout *bravo* (well done, old chap) at its conclusion. (Though only if one is absolutely sure that it has indeed ended, as it is social death to make any sound mid-performance.) But do remember that this is a foreign word, and that one should be yelling *brava* (well done, madam) to female performers or *bravi* (jolly good show, all of you) if addressing a group. You may also throw in the occasional *bravissimo* or *bravissimi* (exceptionally good show) but do not move on to the likes of *magnifico* unless you are prepared for the court of public opinion to find you guilty of showing off.

The other major operatic languages are German, Russian, French, English and Czech. Pause for a moment to consider the delightful absurdity of *Carmen,* an opera set in a Spanish cigarette factory and bullring, being sung in French adorned with English surtitles. If you are in the UK and yearn to hear foreign operas sung in English, English National Opera (ENO) at the London Coliseum is the place for you. Though you should consider that some of the beauty of the vocal line may be lost in translation, and that non-native performers may still not deliver the words in intelligible form. (The impenetrable utterances of an Austrian *soprano* attempting to sing *Turandot* in English still stick in the mind, many years on.) The clinching argument for the victory of surtitles over translation is surely the fact that ENO itself now uses them at every performance, even of works originally written in English.

IS IT WORTH IT?

The most expensive seats at Covent Garden's Royal Opera House (ROH) cost £225 each in 2018, while at Glyndebourne they are £260. At ENO, they are a less eye-watering £125, which is entering the realm of comparability with the cost of a top musical or a Premiership football match. The true madness of the economics of opera production only becomes evident when one considers that the ROH receives little more than 50% of its income from ticket sales, with the remainder coming from government subsidies and charitable donations, while ENO is said to receive about double the money in grants that it takes at the box office.

When this book first appeared five years ago the great Continental opera houses seemed to offer somewhat better value, and that remains the case at the Vienna Staatsoper, with a top ticket price of €205 (£182), but a best-in-the-house seat for *Aida* at Milan's La Scala in 2018 will now set you back €490 (£435), and they can't even pin the blame on Brexit. Plus, if you don't happen to be a native, you have to factor in the not inconsiderable additional costs of travel and accommodation.

All this may make opera seem a hobby only for the rich and privileged, and as a self-respecting bluffer recounting your many experiences of the ROH, you should certainly never betray even a hint of having sat anywhere other than the grand tier or orchestra stalls. But you can find a seat or a standing place for an opera at the ROH for as little as £6 (though those who suffer from vertigo would be well advised to take a rope to lash themselves to some nearby ironwork to preserve their peace of mind).

A mere £6 to reach the highest peak of civilisation – who could possibly begrudge that? Abandon your inhibitions and dip your toe in the comforting and largely shark-free water of grand opera. There is every chance that you will be clamouring for full immersion before too long.

OPERA CHOICE

Let's suppose that you are now ready to cast your prejudices aside and make your first visit to an opera without coercion or inducement by a representative of the corporate hospitality industry. In other words, it is entirely your own decision. What you need now is some sound practical advice on how to bluff about your choice of production, and on where best to go.

WHICH OPERA TO CHOOSE?

The novice is well advised to focus on the classic purveyors of big tunes and simple plots: Mozart, Verdi and Puccini. Wagner does big tunes, too, but to begin there is like dipping your toe into the waters above Niagara when you could have selected a calm English pond.

There is no need to feel defensive about making such a safe choice. Even the greatest opera expert on the planet is unlikely to take strong issue if, having chosen it for your first taste of the musical art form, you assert that Mozart's *The Marriage of Figaro* is the greatest opera ever written. If you really want to impress with your breadth of knowledge, hint that you have also seen the other *Marriage of Figaro* by Marcos Portugal.

If asked how this production of *Figaro* compares with the others you claim to have seen, simply spread your hands and shake your head: how can you possibly choose from among so many? Unless, that is, you have picked up clear signals from other members of the audience that you are witnessing an absolute 24-carat turkey. Deep sighs and outbursts of unintended laughter usually provide a pretty good clue to this; swathes of empty seats after the interval are another.

Your reaction to this should depend on whether your fellow patrons are reacting to musical incompetence or cutting-edge design and direction. The former is easy enough to spot if you go for a work with well-known tunes and have even half an idea how they are supposed to sound. For example, imagine that you have foolishly acquired tickets for the worst-ever performance of *La Bohème* by an obscure touring company from the former Soviet Union. The melodies are familiar enough for you to spot quite quickly that the principal tenor has emerged from the Eric Morecambe school of music: he sings 'all the right notes, but not necessarily in the right order'. He also has the stage presence of a plank that has sagged off to the pub halfway through its first acting lesson in the timber yard, and has failed even to master the thespian's top tip of not bumping into the furniture.

If matched by a similar level of ineptitude across the company, this might make for an evening of genuine hilarity, like the 1970s performances of the Portsmouth

Sinfonia. But sadly, it turns out that the other singers and all the orchestral players actually have a fair idea of what they are supposed to be doing. You will soon find that what you are chiefly sharing with them and the rest of the audience is a profound feeling of sadness at the loss of time and money now gone forever.

There is no harm in being outraged by this sort of thing, though allowances should be made if you are attending a performance by your local amateur operatic company or a school.

The appropriate reaction to a dreadful production is more difficult to gauge. Such affronts to good sense have increased in number over the years. Back in the 1970s, watching Scottish Opera in the north of England (in those halcyon decades when it was an annual visitor to Newcastle Theatre Royal before its regular slot was taken by Opera North in 1997), classic productions were the norm, set in the periods that the opera's authors intended: *Il Trovatore* was full of recognisable gypsies banging on anvils, while *La Traviata* was performed in gorgeous period dress (rather a lot of it in the case of the well-upholstered British soprano Rita Hunter, demanding a considerable suspension of disbelief when she purported to be wasting away from tuberculosis, though the idea that she was 'dying of consumption' was, ironically, entirely credible).

You will easily spot the angle of the director as soon as the curtain goes up. If the cast are wafting around in powdered wigs and crinolines in a plausible simulacrum of a National Trust drawing room, you are probably about to witness a classic production. If they are naked, wearing body paint or jeans, and building the set with sticky tape as they go along, cutting edge is almost certainly what you are in for. The latter is fine, one may reasonably contend, if you have already seen a traditional version of the opera and can therefore understand the conventions that the director is challenging.

'It's a brilliantly refreshing take on this staid old piece, don't you think?' and 'What utter bollocks. Do you fancy a pint?' are equally valid responses.

Your own reactions should be measured according to the company you are keeping. 'It's a brilliantly refreshing take on this staid old piece, don't you think?' and 'What utter bollocks. Do you fancy a pint?' are equally valid responses. It is usually safest to judge yours depending on whether your companion for the evening is wearing a look of wide-eyed enthusiasm or utter despair as you emerge at the interval.

WHERE TO GO?

There has never been a greater range of opportunities to enjoy opera. Let us consider the dazzling range of possibilities in turn.

At home. At the risk of stating the bleeding obvious, it is usually a good idea to practise pretty much anything, from tying a bow-tie to playing the xylophone, in the privacy of one's own home before attempting it in public. Opera need not be an exception, given the ready availability of downloads, CDs and DVDs of the greatest performances of all the best-loved operas (plus a load that no one likes very much, but are constrained by a sense of cultural inferiority from saying so).

If you're 'not sure whether I'd like opera' buy a cheap DVD from a second-hand shop, or borrow it from a library (if you can locate a surviving one) and give it a play. For added authenticity, you may get mildly drunk at the same time. If you truly find that you would rather listen to someone running their fingernails down a blackboard, then perhaps indeed opera is not for you. Either that or your DVD player is kaput. But at least you will have saved yourself a journey and a fair bit of cash by making this discovery in your own mansion, cottage, flat, houseboat or caravette.

If you merely wake up in your chair an hour or two after the performance has finished, with no particular sense of having suffered pain, you may account it a success and consider progressing to the next stage of your induction.

In the cinema. One of the most positive developments of recent years has been the ability to enjoy world-class opera in the comfort and convenience of a huge range of local cinemas, either streamed live from the opera house or recorded for later screening. Consciousness of its reliance on public subsidy, to which all taxpayers contribute, has no doubt been a major driver of the widespread desire to widen access and demonstrate that opera is not just for the urban elite of the world's capitals and other great cities. This means, for example, that you can now watch live performances from the British Royal Opera House and the Met in New York at cinemas across the UK. Not only does this save a fortune on tickets and travel, but at least one director believes it is proving key to 'saving opera for a new generation', as cinematic close-ups discourage the sort of 'hammy over-acting' for which old-style opera used to be renowned.

In total, the Met boasts that its live HD opera transmissions can be enjoyed on more than 2,000 screens in over 70 countries around the world, while the 2017/18 season of Britain's Royal Opera reached over 1,500 cinemas across 40 countries. You can also watch Glyndebourne performances at the cinema, without dressing up, preparing a picnic or travelling to Sussex. Which is seriously good news for those who regard the main attraction as the singing rather than the browsing, sluicing and showing off.

At the theatre. Opera is staged at a much wider range of venues than grand opera houses. In Britain, companies such as Opera North, Welsh National Opera, the Glyndebourne Tour, English Touring Opera, Scottish Opera and NI Opera bring excellent productions to theatres throughout the country, at ticket prices that are perfectly reasonable by general theatrical and sporting standards. And performances are by no means confined to theatres: Scottish Opera, for example, also performs in community centres, schools and village halls, reaching more than 35 communities across Scotland every year.

London offers the choice of the world-class Royal Opera House and English National Opera. The latter charges around half the price of the former, though it would be hard to argue that the ROH is consistently twice as good.

Opera Holland Park, London's third opera house, offers an attractive alternative. A summer opera company, it stages an annual season of opera performances under a temporary canopy in the leafy environs of the eponymous park.

Country-house opera. Then there is England's peculiar contribution to musical culture: the summer festival of country-house opera. Invented by the eccentric John Christie, who in 1934 tacked a small opera house on to his Sussex pile at Glyndebourne, this first spawned flattering imitators at Garsington in Oxfordshire (now transplanted to Wormsley Park in Buckinghamshire) and then at The Grange in Hampshire. In 2017, following a difference of opinion with its landlords, Grange Park Opera relocated itself to the newly built 'Theatre in the Woods' at West Horsley Place in Surrey, leaving summer opera to continue in Hampshire as The Grange Festival. Other aspirants include Longborough Festival Opera in Gloucestershire, Bampton Classical Opera in Oxfordshire and Nevill Holt Opera in Leicestershire, which will also benefit from the opening of a new, purpose-built theatre in 2018.

The economics of building an opera house that is only used for a few weeks every year seem challenging. It either stands idle or, in the case of Garsington, is physically dismantled and put into storage until the next season. Glyndebourne hosts a short autumn season by its own Tour before it embarks on its provincial peregrination. Clonter stages spring and autumn gala performances by talented young singers which can be highly recommended as an introduction to both popular arias and lesser-known works that are often undeserving of their obscurity.

It is worth noting, incidentally, that nearly all of these stage performances in theatres, either permanent or temporary, have the crucial benefit of a roof. Only Bampton takes the risk of performing outdoors in a deanery garden. The widespread perception that it is not worth pitching up to a country-house opera if it happens to be raining is therefore completely incorrect, though the bluffer may wish to use this to his or her advantage either to relieve the ignorant of their tickets or as a convenient excuse for not delivering on a promised summer treat.

Opera houses of the world. There are opera houses on every continent save Antarctica. Virtually every national capital in Europe boasts an opera house, along with many regional centres. They are also well spread across the Americas: in the United States, in the late 19th century, building an opera house became the urban status symbol of choice, to announce a town's prosperity to the world. The bluffer will certainly wish to boast of the great performances he or she has enjoyed at L'Opera, La Scala, the Staatsoper or La Fenice, probably without ever visiting any of them, so here is a handy guide to some of the best (and most obscure).

Country	Opera house	Key bluffing points
Argentina	Teatro Colón, Buenos Aires	Ranked among the greatest opera houses of the world for both architecture and acoustics, the theatre was opened in 1908 and can claim to have hosted many of the greatest opera singers and conductors of the 20th century. Just don't mention the Falklands.
Australia	Sydney Opera House	Designed by a Dane, covered in Swedish tiles, and famously resembling a yacht race, this World Heritage Site was built on the site of a former tram depot and the epic saga of rows and corruption attending the construction of this 'multi-venue peforming arts centre' has even provided the plot for its very own opera: The Eighth Wonder.
Austria	Vienna Staatsoper	Originally the Vienna Court Opera, it opened in 1869 with a performance of Mozart's *Don Giovanni* attended by the Habsburg Emperor Franz Josef, and was reconstructed after extensive bomb damage in Second World War. Today it claims to be the busiest opera house in the world, with up to 60 operas in repertory each year. It also hosts perhaps the world's grandest annual ball. White tie and tails, while obligatory at the ball, are not required to attend performances.

Country	Opera house	Key bluffing points
Brazil	Teatro Amazonas, Manaus	This splendid Renaissance opera house opened in 1897, with a performance of Ponchielli's *La Gioconda*, and played a key role in the gloriously barmy 1982 film *Fitzcarraldo*. In the days before CGI, director Werner Herzog shot the scenes of a 320-ton steamship being hauled over a steep hill by actually doing just that.
Egypt	Cairo Opera House	Successor to the Khedivial Opera House opened in 1869 with a performance of Verdi's *Rigoletto*, and where *Aida* received its world premiere in 1871, and which burned down exactly a century later. Although the Opera House was commissioned to celebrate the opening of the Suez Canal, *Aida* was not (Verdi did not write to order). The current replacement opera house of 1988 was part of the National Cultural Centre and was funded by the Japanese, but opened with Kabuki rather than *Butterfly*.
France	Palais Garnier, Paris	Its décor makes the Palais even better known for opulence than opera, though its chief claim to fame is perhaps as the setting of the novel *The Phantom of the Opera*, turned into an apparently never-ending musical by Andrew Lloyd-Webber in the 1980s. The eight-ton central chandelier in the auditorium has not plummeted on to the audience as yet, but the death of a patron under a falling counterweight in 1896 did provide a light-bulb moment of literary inspiration.

Country	Opera house	Key bluffing points
Germany	Bayreuth Festspielhaus	Designed by Wagner to house a festival dedicated to Wagner, still run by battling Wagners. If you don't like Wagner, don't go. If you do like Wagner, brace yourself for a ten-year wait to buy tickets by post, or develop lightning keyboard skills for the short online booking window. Even if you haven't been, it's probably safe to go all dreamy-eyed and say that it was the most wonderful experience of your life: no Wagner-lover will ever disagree and non-lovers won't care.
Germany	Staatsoper unter den Linden, Berlin	Reconstructed over ten years after the small hiccough of the Second World War, the former state opera of East Germany has an illustrious history and an extensive repertoire. Then there is Deutsche Oper in the former West Berlin, and Komische Oper back in the East, whose repertoire is by no means exclusively comic. In short, if you can't find an opera you fancy seeing in Berlin, you're probably not going to find one anywhere.
Italy	Teatro alla Scala, Milan	Opened in 1778 with a performance of Antonio Salieri's *Europa riconsciuta* (*Europa revealed*) La Scala has also hosted premieres of many more memorable operas, including some of the greatest works of Rossini, Bellini, Donizetti, Verdi and Puccini. The auditorium is famed for both the quality of its acoustics and its unforgivingly critical audiences: check out the video of Roberto Alagna being booed off the stage in a performance of *Aida*.

Country	Opera house	Key bluffing points
Italy	La Fenice, Venice	Opera began in Venice and The Phoenix has so far risen from the ashes three times, most recently after an arson attack in 1996. Famous for staging the premieres of many great operas by Rossini, Donizetti and Verdi (including *Rigoletto* and *La Traviata*), the bluffer should also be aware that it also hosted the premieres of several 20th-century classics including Stravinsky's *The Rake's Progress* and Britten's *The Turn of the Screw* (though not, perversely, his *Death in Venice*).
Italy	Teatro di San Carlo, Naples	The oldest continuously active opera house in the world, opened in 1737, though rebuilt after a disastrous fire in 1816. The 18th century was the golden age of Neapolitan opera, and bluffers may wish to pretend familiarity with composers including Cimarosa, Paisiello and Zingarelli, and should genuinely have heard of Scarlatti. Some of the greatest 19th century composers also wrote operas for Naples: Rossini 10, Donizetti 16 and Verdi 2.
Russia	Bolshoi Theatre, Moscow	Opened in 1825, the Bolshoi staged the premieres of many Russian classic operas by Tchaikovsky, Mussorgsky and Rachmaninoff. It narrowly escaped demolition as a supreme symbol of bourgeois decadence after the Bolshevik revolution, though its full 'Tsar quality' was only recaptured through a six-year post-Soviet restoration, completed in 2011.

Country	Opera house	Key bluffing points
Russia	Mariinsky Theatre, St Petersburg	Notable premieres at the Mariinsky after its opening in 1860 included Mussorgsky's *Boris Godunov*, Borodin's *Prince Igor* and Tchaikovsky's *The Queen of Spades*. Renamed the Kirov after an assassinated local communist leader, it reverted to its original name when Leningrad was also consigned to history. For the last 30 years its artistic reputation has been strongly underpinned by the leadership of the great director and conductor Valery Gergiev.
Sweden	Drottningholms Slottsteater, Stockholm	A baroque time capsule, opened in 1776 and then closed and perfectly preserved after the death of King Gustav III 20 years later. Revived in the 20th century it provides a unique opportunity to stage period operas using authentic 18th-century stage machinery and special effects. This also means the audience sitting on hard wooden baroque benches and doing without other modern conveniences such as air conditioning, but as a bluffer you will confirm that the pain soon passes and is well worth it.
UK	Glyndebourne	Opened in 1994 with a performance of *The Marriage of Figaro*, just as the original theatre attached to the Christie's family home had done exactly 60 years earlier. Don't fail to take your guests into the Organ Room and tell them how the now non-functioning organ brought down a chunk of the ceiling when it was first played; and point out the two pug statues in the garden on your way to picnic by the ha-ha.

Country	Opera house	Key bluffing points
UK	London Coliseum	Designed by the Edwardian legend Frank Matcham, this is the largest theatre in London with 2,359 seats and was originally designed for spectacular variety shows, with a revolving stage to accommodate chariot races. An implausible legend had it that a mechanical malfunction once led to horses crashing through the wall of the pub next door. It has been the home of opera in English since 1968.
UK	Royal Opera House	The shallow treads of the grand staircase were designed for the comfort of ladies in crinolines, which were all the rage when the theatre was rebuilt in 1858; and the balustrade down the middle was intended to stop them becoming entangled when they passed on the stairs. You should also mention casually that the dome above the auditorium is made of papier-maché.
UK	The Theatre in the Woods	The new home of Grange Park Opera in Surrey holds the world record for fastest construction of an opera house: a proper five-storey auditorium modelled on La Scala (q.v.) erected in just one year after £8m of fundraising, on an estate unexpectedly inherited by sometime University Challenge host Bamber Gascoigne. A pleasant mile's stroll from the nearest railway station or reachable by shuttle bus or vintage Rolls-Royce. Set in the formal gardens of a 15th-century house where opera-goers may dine in the long interval.

Country	Opera house	Key bluffing points
USA	Civic Opera House, Chicago	The home of the distinguished Lyric Opera company since it was founded in 1954, this Art Deco theatre of 1929 is the second largest opera house in North America and presents a fine programme of both classic and contemporary works. Every bluffer should know that Lyric Opera is famous both for the American debut of Maria Callas in its very first season, and for barring Luciano Pavarotti after his 26th cancellation of a performance in 1989.
USA	Winspear Opera House, Dallas	Bill Winspear, a Canadian who built a successful business in Dallas, gave $42 million to fulfil his dream 'that Dallas will have great opera, and that our Opera will help Dallas to become one of the great cities of the world'. In true operatic style he died two years before the theatre opened in 2009. Its $5m retracting chandelier shows great promise of becoming as famous as the one in Paris's Palais Garnier, though it has yet to catch the eye of Andrew Lloyd Webber. The resident Dallas Opera company, founded in 1957, previously staged the US debuts of many distinguished singers including Monserrat Caballé, Plácido Domingo and Joan Sutherland, and of the director and designer Franco Zeffirelli.

Country	Opera house	Key bluffing points
USA	Alice Busch Opera Theater, Glimmerglass	The lakeside Glimmerglass Festival in upstate New York is perhaps the nearest thing the US has to offer to an English country-house opera experience, with the difference that ticket prices start at $26 (before a range of community discounts), the dining opportunities are before or after rather than during the performance, and the sartorial code is 'dress for your comfort, and enjoy the show'. The result is a collection of TripAdvisor reviews that any celebrity chef or hotelier would kill for: might this provide the plot for an exciting modern opera?
USA	Metropolitan Opera, New York	Founded in 1880, the Met has been housed since 1966 at the Lincoln Center, where its 3,800 seats make the London Coliseum look like a hick town fleapit. A pioneer in widening access to opera through radio, TV and live HD broadcasts in cinemas, the Met arguably has the greatest reach of any opera company in the world. While it has, as you would expect, staged premieres of operas by distinguished US composers Samuel Barber and Philip Glass, no bluffer should lose an opportunity to mention that it also premiered two works by Puccini: *La Fanciulla del West* and *Il Trittico*.

Country	Opera house	Key bluffing points
USA	War Memorial Opera House, San Francisco	The home of San Francisco Opera since 1932, and also the venue for the signing of the United Nations Charter in 1945: surely it is only a matter of time before someone writes an opera about that. Those 49er miners apparently loved their opera as much as they lusted after gold: San Francisco staged nearly 5,000 performances in 26 different theatres between 1851 and the great earthquake of 1906. Proximity to the San Andreas fault must also have added a unique frisson to the 2018 performances of Wagner's *Götterdämmerung*.
USA	Sheridan Opera House, Colorado	Opened in 1913 to serve the silver mining town of Telluride, now reinvented as a ski resort and film festival venue. Bonus bluffing points can be gained by casually mentioning that Telluride was the scene of Butch Cassidy's first recorded bank robbery in 1889.
Vietnam	Hanoi Opera House	Constructed by the French colonial administration and modelled on the Palais Garnier in Paris, the theatre opened in 1911 and its own website concedes that it now needs to be 'upgraded and renovated'. Visitors are more likely to encounter a Vietnamese musical or opera, or classical music or ballet, than a Western opera. For many, this will no doubt be a relief.

Then there are festivals running through the alphabet from Aix-en-Provence to Wexford, via Bregenz (featuring a dramatic floating stage on Lake Constance) and Verona (presenting the grandest productions of popular operas in an authentic Roman arena). You should feel free to drop the names of any of these into interval conversations as evidence of the breadth of your operatic experience, perhaps steering clear only of Verona on account of its populist programming and the correspondingly increased chance that you will find yourself talking to someone who has actually been there.

If you are based in the UK, the best advice is to start with a decent touring opera company and, if you feel so inclined, work your way up from there. But never be deterred by people telling you that 'you can't get tickets' for anything that takes your fancy. It is true that the booking system at the Royal Opera House (ROH) would make even a senior Byzantine civil servant feel in need of a lie-down, and that members snap up the best tickets at the major country-house opera festivals up to nine months before they start. But, as a result, a decent number of tickets are then returned by those who find that they cannot actually attend on the date in question because they are now dead, giving birth or have been posted overseas. A little perseverance on the telephone to the box office nearly always yields a positive result.

On the other hand, if you don't actually want to go, the conventional claim that you 'can't get tickets' should satisfy your would-be guest, unless he or she has also read this book.

HOUSE ETIQUETTE

WHEN TO ARRIVE?

The first and most important rule of opera-going is: be punctual. Most opera houses will not admit latecomers 'until a suitable break in the performance', if at all. That could mean blowing £300 on a couple of tickets to watch the opera relayed on a TV screen in the bar, if you are lucky. Bearing in mind the legendary unreliability of public transport, and the unpredictability of traffic, it is wise to aim to arrive half an hour before curtain up and spend the time enjoying a fortifying drink and studying the synopsis in the programme. Although the advent of surtitles makes such homework less essential than it was in days gone by, it is always a good idea to arrive before your guests and impress them with the knowledge you acquired two minutes earlier.

WHAT TO WEAR?

The simple truth at most British venues is: wear pretty much anything you like. Though you can, if you wish, have great fun inventing non-existent rules for novices, such as persuading them that it's de rigueur to turn up at the ROH in white tie and tails.

In 1998 the then incoming chairman of the ROH, Sir Colin Southgate, got into terrible trouble for announcing: 'I don't want to sit next to somebody with a singlet, smelly shorts and a pair of trainers when I go to the opera. I'm a relaxed guy. I'm not wearing a tie. But there are standards.'

Not any more there aren't – not with today's universal emphasis on widening access. Though at Glyndebourne, Garsington and Grange Park Opera, where black tie is 'customary but not obligatory', turning up in jeans and trainers will still mark you down as either (a) an irrepressible free spirit, or (b) a bit of a prat.

There was a time when one felt able to assert with confidence that 'you can't overdress for Glyndebourne'. Yet even 20 years ago a certain froideur might arise when a young lady followed that advice and turned up in a flowing ball gown, only to find nearly every other female (and some rather odd men) in the sort of day dress that would not arouse comment in the average office. But if you're the sort of lady who enjoys dressing up, there is much to be said for simply going for it and aiming to drag everyone else's standards back up with you. (Oddly enough, while Garsington and Grange Park Opera may not quite match the world-class standards of Glyndebourne's opera, they do on the whole attract a rather smarter class of punter.) In the wider world, it is prudent to consult the website of your chosen theatre to see whether a local dress code applies. At La Fenice in

Venice, for example, a tuxedo is 'recommendable' for the opening night of the season, while for other premieres 'ladies need to wear a black dress, gentlemen jacket and tie'. For matinees, the 'dress code is fairly relaxed, smart-casual, but PLEASE, people wearing shorts or sleeveless T-shirts will not be allowed inside the auditorium; in this case, tickets will not be reimbursed.' Don't say you weren't warned.

HOW TO BEHAVE?

The first rule of opera is silence. Do not bring in a box of chocolates, unwrap them noisily and hand them along the row. Do not imagine that, just because only the orchestra is playing and no one has actually started singing, it is all right to continue your conversation with your companions. If you cannot sit quietly through 90 minutes in a theatre without noisily slurping on a bottle of water, perhaps you might consider returning to your mother and asking to be properly weaned. The only time that it is appropriate to make a sound is (a) if you notice that the theatre is on fire, and (b) at the conclusion of an act or a particularly outstanding aria, when you may applaud and/or utter a few appropriate Italian words (not including 'Mamma mia' and 'spaghetti alle vongole').

The only class of person exempt from these (and all other) rules is the sort of indomitable British battleaxe who, as a letter writer to the *Daily Telegraph* recounted in 2012, is liable to respond to a polite request to 'shush' with a glare and a loud instruction to 'shush yourself!'. Such exploits always give great pleasure to the readers of obituaries, though they seem considerably less amusing when encountered in real life.

It surely hardly needs saying that leaving your mobile phone ringtone switched on during a performance is social suicide. But perhaps it is worth adding that sneaking the phone out of your pocket for a crafty look at the screen to check your e-mails or the cricket score, or to play a game or two during the duller bits of the show, is almost equally distracting to your neighbours and completely unacceptable. To the point where the person seated next to you would be perfectly entitled to snatch the phone from you and jump up and down on it when the curtain next falls.

WHAT TO EAT AND DRINK?

There is no necessary connection between the opera and food and drink. After sleeping through more than an hour of an eagerly awaited performance of *Götterdämmerung* thanks to an injudiciously well-lubricated lunch, it can be asserted with some authority that excessive alcohol detracts as much from performance in the opera house as it does in the bedroom. On the other hand, the bloke in the next seat did thoughtfully whisper, 'You lucky sod: you haven't missed much.'

Having said that, a refreshing glass of something fizzy is always welcome before the curtain rises or at the interval. The centrepiece of the country-house opera is a 90-minute interval in which one can consume a picnic on the lawn (or thoughtfully provided marquee, if wet) or eat a perfectly decent (if far from cheap) meal in a restaurant. Please do not be tempted to light a barbecue on the main lawn at Glyndebourne, though, unless you wish to be savaged to death by Dennis and Ian, the two pugs owned by current chairman Gus Christie. Those collapsible tables modelled on the ones found in pub beer gardens are best avoided too, given their propensity to collapse at moments of their own choosing rather than their owner's.

If paying a first visit to an English country-house opera, it is wise to impress upon the person responsible for the catering that the interval is a longish period and that they should be thinking in terms of a three-course meal rather than a poolside snack. There have been unfortunate and relationship-straining instances where, in the absence of proper instructions, ladies have interpreted 'a picnic' for Glyndebourne as comprising two individual pork pies, a Scotch egg and a couple of apples.

It is also a good idea to plan ahead when assembling all the ingredients for a successful picnic, including an appropriate hamper or other container in which to convey them to your chosen spot. You are unlikely ever to attain the depths of embarrassment that one gentleman suffered some years ago when he asked to borrow a cool box from a dear friend in the veterinary profession, making him surely the only person in history to have tried to walk nonchalantly across the lawns at Glyndebourne carrying a white polystyrene box emblazoned on each side in large red letters: 'Semen: Handle With Care'.

WHAT TO SAY?

As already noted, during the performance: nothing. After the show, 'Wasn't it absolutely marvellous?' will usually get you a long way. Failing that, try lobbing in a bit of technical babble, such as 'Didn't you feel that the *soprano* was a bit insecure above the stave?' This line used to feature in reviews with great regularity, yet only a previous edition of this guide ever deigned to explain that it signifies one who is inclined to wobble on the high notes. Now you know too, and may bluff with as much confidence as any other critic.

THE CURTAIN RISES: HOW OPERA STARTED

There can be few human activities whose official starting date and place can be stated with more precision than that of opera: 6 March 1637 in Venice, with the inaugural performance at the world's first commercial opera house.

Of course, some Venetian entrepreneur did not suddenly have a light-bulb moment and announce 'I know just what the world's been waiting for: a phenomenally expensive entertainment where people sing instead of speak, with a large orchestra and spectacular stage effects flung in, including, but not restricted to, flooding of the stage (never too much of a challenge in Venice), flying machines, thunder and lightning, and maybe a spot of ballet. On horseback! Nurse, the screens!'

No, as previously noted, the notion had been brewing for centuries through the evolution of religious plays with musical interludes, illustrating aspects of the Bible, particularly the Christmas and Easter stories. Originally performed in church, these gradually evolved into outdoor entertainment, no doubt to accommodate medieval demand for a proto-Glyndebourne experience on a picnic rug.

The opera craze swept Venice like a plague, though with somewhat happier results.

By the 15th century, such diversions had spread into the unmistakably secular sphere, with many members of the Italian nobility considering that a performance by singers and instrumentalists at their weddings was as indispensable as a chocolate fountain would be in Gateshead in 2010. The Medicis of Florence were particularly keen, with the performance no doubt conveniently diverting attention from the enhancement with poison of the drinks belonging to select guests.

The entertainment at the 1589 wedding of Ferdinando de' Medici, Grand Duke of Tuscany, proved such a success that it was said to be the inspiration for the first recorded opera, *Dafne*, in 1597 (recorded, in the sense of someone making a note that it had happened, rather than pitching up with a very early prototype of the phonograph). In 1600, its composer, Jacopo Peri, went on to create the first recognisable opera with a surviving score, *Euridice*.

Much of the blame for the evolution of opera in the late 16th century can be attached to a group called the Florentine Camerata, led by one Count Giovanni de' Bardi, who fondly imagined that they were reviving the traditions of classical Greek drama, with its arguably singing chorus.

Opera's great stroke of luck at this point was the emergence of an indisputable genius, Claudio Monteverdi (1567–1643). He achieved his first big hit with *L'Orfeo* (1607) and went on, in his 70s, to write two of the earliest complete operas still regularly performed: *Il Ritorno d'Ulisse in Patria* (1641) and *L'Incoronazione di Poppea* (1642). Poppea and Nero's concluding love duet, 'Pur ti miro', is unquestionably one of the most beautiful pieces of music ever written (though musicologists now question whether it was actually written by Monteverdi) and a natural choice for the sophisticated bluffer's desert island. It also makes a fine choice as background music for the signing of the register at weddings.

So complete was the development of opera by 1645 that the English diarist John Evelyn could write of a visit to Venice: 'We went to the Opera, where comedies and other plays are represented in recitative music, by the most excellent musicians, vocal and instrumental, with variety of scenes painted and contrived with no less art of perspective, and machines for flying in the air, and other wonderful notions; taken together, it is one of the most magnificent and expensive diversions the wit of man can invent.'

That quotation has been made easier to digest by modernisation of the spelling, which would otherwise have provided the only clue that Evelyn was writing in 1645 as in the year, rather than at a quarter to five this afternoon.

The opera craze swept Venice like a plague, though with somewhat happier results. Opera houses sprang up in virtually every parish, like mushrooms after rain. At least 16 had opened by 1700. To keep them in business, after the sad but hardly premature demise of Monteverdi, there luckily emerged a series of talented local composers, including Francesco Cavalli (1602–1676) whose 41 operas include *La Calisto*, successfully revived at Glyndebourne and elsewhere in modern times. While the bluffer stands little risk of exposure by adopting the widespread view that early opera may be dismissed as obscure, difficult and repetitive, it is in fact tuneful and can be hugely entertaining; this can be stated with some confidence with little risk of inviting ridicule. Just remember to cite the 2008 Royal Opera performance of *La Calisto* as an outstanding example of how good it can be.

The baton of Italian opera was carried forward into the 18th century by the likes of the Neapolitan Alessandro Scarlatti (1660–1725) and the Venetians Tomaso Albinoni (1671–1751) and Antonio Vivaldi (1678–1741). Vivaldi may be chiefly famed by posterity for writing *The Four Seasons* for bank advertisements, and former bad-boy violinist Nigel Kennedy, but he proudly claimed to have written no fewer than 94 operas, a rate of artistic productivity rarely equalled until Ernie Wise's character in the *Morecambe & Wise Show* turned his hand to writing plays.

Meanwhile, in France as in Italy, opera had evolved from the lavish musical entertainment put on for royal weddings, birthdays and state visits, led from the mid-17th century by an imported Florentine, Jean-Baptiste Lully (1632–87). It is entirely typical that the undisputed founder of French opera should not have been French at all. Lully is credited with introducing a number of new instruments to the operatic orchestra and is noted for the important role he accorded to dance. This reflected Lully's own tastes and, no doubt more importantly, those of his patron King Louis XIV. Lully's music provides the acclaimed soundtrack for the 2000 film *Le Roi Danse*.

Lully himself died of gangrene contracted after striking his foot with the long staff with which he was beating time at a performance of his *Te Deum* to celebrate Louis XIV's recovery from illness, a fate which no doubt did much to encourage the development of the altogether less dangerous conductor's baton.

Lully was followed by Jean-Philippe Rameau (1683–1764) who was 50 when he penned his first opera, *Hippolyte et Aricie* (1733), but made up for his slow start with a series of *tragédies en musique* based on classical myths, including *Castor et Pollux* (1737), *Dardanus* (1739) and *Zoroastre* (1749). Like Lully before him, he made extensive use of dance and theatrical special effects, lest the mere singing bored his courtly audience (who probably had somewhat limited attention spans).

Rameau also essayed the comic, notably in *Platée* (1745), the bizarre story of Jupiter's supposed infatuation with the hideous swamp monster of the title. The natural inclination to imagine that Rameau created this role to reflect the large number of suitably qualified French *soprano*s at the time is belied by the fact that it was first performed by a high tenor. It was apparently well received from the start, despite the fact that it would have been hard to pick a less appropriate story than the wooing of a grotesque marsh nymph as the entertainment for the wedding of Louis XV's son and heir – a lad who wasn't exactly an oil painting himself. Its stock soared further on revivals, to the point where Jean-Jacques Rousseau in 1752 could write 'Call it sublime! Never repent of having considered it Rameau's masterpiece and the most excellent work that has ever as yet been heard in our opera house.' And now the best review that a composer can hope for is a mere five stars.

But what, you ask, of England? What was happening in the true centre of the universe while these continentals were prancing around singing in foreign tongues about classical myths? As is so often true of England, it is a case of 'if only'. If only the country had not been preoccupied with waging a civil war, cutting off its king's head and installing an utterly joyless Puritan government that demonstrated its love of life by closing down all the public theatres, opera would no doubt have made an impact considerably more quickly than it did. In 1639 Sir William Davenant obtained a licence to build what would have been the first public opera house anywhere outside Italy, though it took him until 1671 to launch a fitting venue for opera in the splendid Dorset Garden Theatre at Blackfriars, designed by Wren with a proscenium arch adorned by carvings by

Grinling Gibbons. However, Sir William's contribution to the first night party was somewhat muted, as he had died in 1668.

Before he did, though, Davenant had improvised a stage to present what is generally considered the first opera performed in England, *The Siege of Rhodes*. A distinctly brave move in 1656, four years before the Restoration of Charles II. Perhaps Sir William's preference for describing the work as 'Recitative Musick' rather than an opera was an attempt to keep the Puritan thought police off his scent.

And then, as luck would have it, along came a genius. England's Monteverdi was Henry Purcell (1659–95), whose first opera *Dido and Aeneas* was performed in 1689, not at the gorgeous Dorset Garden Theatre but by the young ladies of a girls' school in Chelsea (at least so legend has it, though the bluffer should be aware that contemporary musicologists prefer the more pedestrian theory that it started life as a court masque). Everyone should also have heard of *Dido and Aeneas* because the concluding 'Dido's Lament' is, by common consent, one of those hauntingly beautiful bits of music that has attained immortality and will forever be in demand on 78rpm discs to be played on a wind-up gramophone on a desert island.

Though getting inside a girls' school would be the height of most men's ambitions, Purcell graduated to the more conventional stage with other works that are still regularly performed by opera companies today, most notably *King Arthur* (1691) and *The Fairy Queen* (1692), though both feature spoken dialogue and may therefore be best considered as straight plays with musical interludes rather than operas in the usual sense.

On the other side of the English Channel, the operatic world of the first half of the 18th century was dominated by *opera seria* (serious opera), focusing on the exploits of various gods and ancient heroes – to which the aristocratic audiences who were its target market could naturally relate. At the same time, by way of light relief, there also developed *opera buffa* (comic opera), usually focusing on the contemporary and the everyday.

The earliest *opere buffe* (that's the plural, not a typo) were devised as *intermezzi* to be performed in the intervals between acts of *opere serie* – the 18th-century equivalent of a commercial break, with the advertisements similarly likely to prove more entertaining than the programme one is actually supposed to be watching. The earliest you are likely to come across in a modern production is *La Serva Padrona* (1733) by Pergolesi (1710–36). This provides 45 minutes of entirely predictable fun involving a cast of just three: the crusty, elderly confirmed bachelor Uberto, his cheeky serving wench Serpina and his manservant Vespone. It ends in a wedding.

By the second half of the 18th century, the *opera buffa* had developed a fully fledged life of its own. The key fact the bluffer needs to know is that if it says *opera buffa* on the title page of the programme, it is likely to have a happy ending (if marriage can be considered in that light), whereas *opera seria* will more than likely conclude with a stage piled high with corpses.

In Britain, the supreme exponent of *opera seria* was that great German-born honorary Englishman George

Frideric Handel (1685–1759). Such was the power of his musical genius that he succeeded in making opera in Italian popular among this insular and monoglot people. He turned out more than 40 of them, all packed full of memorable tunes, before turning to focus in the latter part of his career on oratorios.

Few great operatic composers have experienced more massive swings in both expert and popular estimation than Handel. A critical and box-office success in his own day, his operatic works vanished from the repertory for the best part of 200 years after his death. To take an extreme example, *Poro, Rè dell'Indie* was unperformed in London between 1731 and 1998.

The latter 20th century happily rediscovered an appetite for staged Handel that could not be satisfied even by the huge number of operas he had actually written, and many oratorios from *Semele* to *Theodora* and even *Messiah* have been successfully presented as full-blown operas.

There is a strong case, if one has to be cast away with the music of just one composer, for choosing Handel. There are few more beautiful arias than 'Ombra Mai Fù' from *Xerxes*, few sexier than 'Endless Pleasure' from *Semele*, few more moving than 'As With Rosy Steps the Morn' from *Theodora*. No bluffer should hesitate to acknowledge Handel's brilliance or to bask in the balm of his music.

When asked for the secret of La Bohème's appeal, Britain's King George V simply replied: 'It's the shortest one I know.'

THE BIG ARIA: THE GREAT OPERA COMPOSERS

If you want to bluff successfully about opera, it is essential to know about the four composers already mentioned. The mainstay of the standard repertoire, Mozart, Verdi, Wagner and Puccini, are a more or less cast-iron guarantee of good box-office sales. (The rather narrower appeal of Wagner is amply offset by the greater fanaticism of his followers, ensuring that performances of his demanding works tend to sell out even more rapidly than more accessible offerings from the others.)

WOLFGANG AMADEUS MOZART (1756–91)

Many of us know about Mozart from the play or film *Amadeus*: the amazing child prodigy turned foul-mouthed youth who in just 35 years composed some of the world's best-loved operas as well as a staggering number of symphonies, concertos, masses and other works, before he was cleverly murdered by his jealous rival Antonio Salieri.

The four operas that any bluffer really needs to know about are the three composed in collaboration with the librettist Lorenzo da Ponte – *The Marriage of Figaro* (1786), *Don Giovanni* (1787) and *Così fan Tutte* (1790) – plus a form of German music-drama known as *singspiel, The Magic Flute* (1791).

The Marriage of Figaro

Do not walk into a performance of *Le Nozze di Figaro* (the Italian name for the opera) knowledgeably humming that tune about 'Figaro, Figaro, Figaro' that will be lurking in the recesses of your memory. That is from the later *Il Barbiere di Siviglia* (The Barber of Seville) by Gioachino Rossini (and *Classic Advertisements Vol 3*). Both operas contain the same characters and are based on plays by French playwright Beaumarchais. Mozart's audiences would have been familiar with earlier events in the lives of Figaro, Count Almaviva, Doctor Bartolo and his ward Rosina (now the Countess Almaviva) from the 1782 version of *Il Barbiere di Siviglia* by Giovanni Paisiello.

By the time of *Le Nozze di Figaro,* the erstwhile barber has gone to work as valet to the Count, who is attracted to Figaro's wife-to-be Susanna and regrets his decision to give up his feudal *droit de seigneur*. In a single day of madness Figaro and Susanna outwit the Count at every turn and end up not only happily married but with the Count begging forgiveness from his ill-used wife. A joyous evening out, the work features some of the greatest music of all time, and was certainly a brave choice to stage in an opera house full of counts.

Don Giovanni

Don Giovanni is about another nobleman gone bad, a notorious philanderer whose conquests his manservant has noted in a little black book, brought out for the famous 'catalogue aria' in which he announces his master's total in Spain as 1,003. Although billed as an *opera buffa*, it kicks off with an attempted rape and a murder and concludes, satisfactorily enough, when the mocked statue of the murder victim, the Commendatore, accepts Don Giovanni's invitation to dinner and drags him off to his well-deserved comeuppance in hell.

Così fan Tutte

Having twice offended aristocrats, Mozart turned his attention to the ladies in *Così fan Tutte* (Thus Do All Women), another *opera buffa* in which a cynical older man, Don Alfonso, seeks to prove to two idealistic young soldiers, who are happily engaged to two sisters, that women are constitutionally incapable of fidelity. To settle a wager, the two pretend to go off to war and return lightly disguised as Albanians. Each woos the sister of his fiancée. Egged on by their perky maid Despina, the sisters succumb and marry the newcomers. Cue martial music and the return of their original fiancés. An undoubted musical treat, modern productions tend to find it hard to accept that everyone is going to have a good laugh about this and live happily ever after. The male bluffer will do well to acknowledge the shocking premise of the opera in female company, while also keeping very quiet about the fact that he has spent much of the performance speculating which woman, Fiordiligi, Dorabella or Despina, he would choose to dally with first if the opportunity arose.

The Magic Flute

A baffling fantasy, this one involves a bird-catcher (Papageno) and a prince (Tamino) on a mission to rescue the Queen of the Night's daughter (Pamina) from a baddie (Sarastro) who in fact turns out to be a goodie after all. Being a *singspiel* rather than an opera, it uses spoken dialogue between the arias, which are definitely worth waiting for: if they have found a *soprano* who can actually hit the implausible high notes, the Queen of the Night's famous aria can make any bluffer's evening. If asked what on earth it was all about, it is safe to murmur that it is an allegory on freemasonry, then move swiftly on.

Mozart wrote 18 other operas, from *La Finta Semplice* (1768), which is really pretty good for the work of a 12-year-old, to *La Clemenza di Tito* (1791) written in the last year of his life. The latter is regularly performed, along with *Mitridate, re di Ponto* (1770), *Idomeneo* (1781) and *Die Entführung aus dem Serail* (1782). All fill an evening perfectly pleasantly (though, in the case of the latter, any operas set in harems and involving abductions by Turkish pashas are generally best avoided where possible); but for true satisfaction the bluffer should stick to the three great da Ponte operas.

GIUSEPPE VERDI (1813–1901)

Verdi cuts an altogether more romantic figure in Italian than he would translated as Joe Green. An improbable fact for pub quiz aficionados is that this greatest of Italians and hero of the *Risorgimento* movement for Italian unification was in fact born in France, albeit only because the Duchy of Parma had been annexed by Napoleon at the time.

Verdi cuts an altogether more romantic figure in Italian than he would translated as Joe Green.

After the tragic deaths of his infant children and young wife, and the apparent failure of his first two operas, Verdi achieved success with *Nabucco* (1842) and was still at the top of the operatic tree more than 50 years later when he wrote *Falstaff* (1893). The other works by which he is best known include *Macbeth* (1847), *Rigoletto* (1851), *Il Trovatore* and *La Traviata* (both 1853), *Simon Boccanegra* (1857/1881), *Un Ballo in Maschera* (1859), *Don Carlos* (1867), *Aida* (1871) and *Otello* (1887). Those with plots borrowed from Shakespeare offer obvious advantages for those old enough to have been educated in England when such hard stuff featured on the curriculum. But the plots of Verdi operas are usually pretty simple compared with those of his exact contemporary Wagner, who enjoyed the same sort of relationship with the Nordic gods that Tolkien had with elves.

With Verdi, one can usually rely on a comprehensible melodrama involving real people, ending with one or more dead bodies on the stage and featuring a host of really good tunes along the way. Even the sort of people who think they hate opera will cheerfully hum along to the 'Chorus of the Hebrew Slaves' from *Nabucco,* 'La Donna è Mobile' ('The Woman is Fickle') from *Rigoletto,* the 'Drinking Song' from *La Traviata* or the 'Grand March' from *Aida.*

No bluffer should fall for the schoolboy error of claiming that *Aida* was written to celebrate the opening of the Suez Canal, but it was commissioned by the Khedive of Egypt and had its premiere at the Cairo Opera House on Christmas Eve 1871. Like *Nabucco,* it is performed less frequently than one might expect, given the familiarity and greatness of its music, presumably because of the very substantial resources required to stage it properly. The opportunity to attend a performance by a competent opera company should therefore never be lightly turned down, even if one has to trek to the arena in Verona for the occasion.

None of Verdi's less familiar operas will offend the ear or bore the observer – or at any rate not to excess. The Royal Opera in the 1990s made a brave attempt to perform the entire Verdi canon, either fully staged or in concert, allowing this to be asserted with reasonable confidence. Though the appearance of unfamiliar names did have some mildly amusing side effects: some keen operagoers thought they had been invited to a performance of *Otello* and were distinctly bemused by the absence of the Moor and his wife from *Attila* (1846), a jolly three-acter about the rape and pillage of the Italian peninsula by the eponymous Hun.

RICHARD WAGNER (1813–83)

The world is neatly divided into those who adore Wagner and those who loathe him: consequently, pretending indifference is not really an option for the bluffer.

One good word to bandy around if feigning adoration is 'leitmotiv' (pronounced 'lite'-motiv), which refers to the recurring musical themes associated with particular characters and situations through Wagner's four-act opera cycle of 1853–69 *Der Ring des Nibelugen* (or, more simply, *The Ring*). While no discussion of Wagner is complete without a considerable amount of banging on about leitmotivs, it is handy to know that Wagner disliked the word and never used it himself.

You will also do well to get all misty-eyed about Bayreuth (pronounce it 'By-royt', to avoid any potential confusion with the capital of Lebanon), where the Festspielhaus (Festival Theatre), constructed to Wagner's specifications and still run by his descendants, is dedicated to the performance of his works. Tickets are notoriously hard to obtain, with Wagnerians typically submitting annual applications for a decade before they are successful in the ballot, which is the cue for celebrations more usually associated with winning the lottery.

If affecting to detest Wagner, the key fact to bring up is naturally that Adolf Hitler was a huge fan of his work. Other valid reasons to dislike the man include the inordinate length at which he insisted on writing. His comedy *Die Meistersinger von Nürnberg* lasts a full five-and-a-quarter hours while the four-opera *Ring* occupies at least 15 hours, excluding intervals; even the apparently manageable two-and-a-half-hour *Das Rheingold*, with which *The Ring* kicks off, is rendered uncomfortable for those above a certain age because Wagner insisted that it should be performed without an interval: a positive body blow to theatres that rely on bar takings to bolster their receipts at the box office.

Wagner was big on details like that. Most unusually, he wrote the *libretti* as well as the music for all his works, and even specified the stage directions.

Even some dedicated operagoers come late to Wagner, not least because the mid-afternoon starting times of so many of his operas are not readily compatible with a full-time job. But there is no denying the power of his music, once one sets prejudice or misgivings aside and goes for it. Everyone knows 'Here Comes the Bride' from *Lohengrin* (1850) and part of the *Apocalypse Now* soundtrack 'Ride of the Valkyries' from *Die Walküre* (the second instalment of *The Ring*, 1870), and there are other considerable riches to discover for the bluffer with an iron backside but without a tin ear.

GIACOMO PUCCINI (1858–1924)

Puccini is surely the most tuneful and accessible of the great opera composers. Three of his works – *La Bohème* (1896), *Tosca* (1900) and *Madama Butterfly* (1904) regularly feature towards the top of league tables of the world's most frequently performed operas. This no doubt reflects the fact that Puccini is considerably easier on the bottoms as well as the ears and intellects of the audience than Wagner. *La Bohème* was a particular favourite of Britain's King George V; when asked for the secret of its appeal, he simply replied: 'It's the shortest one I know.' Two hours of fantastic music, plus an interval, then back to the palace (or the pub). Who could ask for more?

La Bohème, a moving tale of love and death in a student garret in Paris, gave the world one of opera's best-loved *arias*: 'Che Gelida Manina' ('Your Tiny Hand is Frozen'); *Tosca* has 'Vissi d'Arte' ('I Lived for Art'); and *Madama Butterfly* has 'Un Bel di Vedremo' ('One Fine Day'). But any bluffer worth his or her salt should also be aware of the hugely popular arias from two of Puccini's less frequently performed operas: 'O Mio Babbino Caro' ('Oh My Beloved Father') from the one-act *Gianni Schicchi* (1918) and the all-time hit parade topper 'Nessun Dorma' ('None Shall Sleep') from *Turandot* (1926). The latter is best known as the theme which accompanied the BBC's TV coverage of the 1990 World Cup, and was described by presenter Des Lynam as 'probably the outstanding theme of any major televised sporting event ever'. Opera purists are still squirming, but as a bluffer you will know better, saying: 'Anything which brings great opera to the people is a good thing.' Then, adopting your best Abe Lincoln expression, gaze benevolently into the far distance.

The attentive reader will have noted that *Turandot* had its premiere two years after the composer died. He left it unfinished, and the final act was completed by Franco Alfano. A good challenge to individuals who swear that they 'do not like opera' is to take them to see the Royal Opera's *Turandot* and see whether they still hold to that view by the time of the final curtain: none has so far. However, similar results should be obtainable from decent performances of any of Puccini's better-known works.

One bluff-worthy feature of Puccini's operas is the preponderance of loathsome characters: Baron Scarpia the evil secret policeman and torturer in *Tosca;* Pinkerton the worthless racist sailor who deserts the doting Cio-Cio-San in *Madama Butterfly*. Though these are perhaps capped by Princess Turandot, who has the slave girl Liù tortured and driven to suicide to protect the secret of her master Calaf's identity; it has been speculated that the strain of steering the plot from here to a happy ending accounted for Puccini's failure to complete the opera.

Less well known but still enjoyable Puccini operas include *Manon Lescaut* (1893), not to be confused with the other *Manon* by Jules Massenet (*see* 'Supporting Chorus: The Also-Rans, page 59); *La Fanciulla del West* (The Girl of the Golden West, 1910), which offers the rare opportunity in Italian grand opera to cast the role of 'Billy Jackrabbit', an American Indian; *La Rondine* (1917); and *Il Trittico* (1918), comprising three one-act operas: the dark *Il Tabarro,* the tragedy *Suor Angelica* and the comedy *Gianni Schicchi,* already mentioned.

SUPPORTING CHORUS: THE ALSO-RANS

While a sketchy knowledge of the great works of Mozart, Verdi, Wagner and Puccini should carry the bluffer a fair way in everyday conversation, there is a considerable number of other composers with whom it is desirable to be acquainted. The difficulty is in knowing where to draw the line.

So far, upwards of 40,000 operas have been written (that we know about), and deluded fools continue to churn them out. Only a tiny minority actually make it to some sort of stage. The vast majority of operas are never performed. Festivals such as Wexford in Ireland exist precisely to discover and revive forgotten operas: occasionally they come up with an absolute gem, though more often they merely demonstrate why a work vanished into obscurity in the first place. No one in their right mind could pretend acquaintance with every opera composer, but the bluffer should at least pretend to have heard of the following, listed in approximate chronological order:

GLUCK (1714–87)

Born in Bavaria, Christoph Willibald von Gluck was a favoured composer of the Habsburg court in Vienna. He secured a lasting place in the operatic repertory with *Orfeo ed Euridice* (1762) and its most famous aria 'Che Farò Senza Euridice?' ('What is Life?'). This was the first of his 'reform' operas, designed to simplify the conventions of *opera seria*. Others that you may also still encounter on stage include *Alceste* (1767), *Iphigénie en Aulide* (1774), *Armide* (1777) and *Iphigénie en Tauride* (1779). It seems idle to deny that Willibald had a bit of a crush on strong women whose names began with 'A'; if they could not meet his absolute ideal of being called Iphigénie. The bluffer should also use any mention of *Armide* to ask 'Which one?' since there is an earlier opera, to the same *libretto*, by Lully.

BEETHOVEN (1770–1827)

The bluffer need know only two key facts about Ludwig van Beethoven: he went deaf, and was more a man for symphonies than operas. But that did not stop him trying, and between 1805 and 1814 he struggled to complete his only opera, *Fidelio,* for which he came up with no fewer than four different overtures. He wrote that the effort would 'win him a martyr's crown' and wisely steered clear of opera afterwards.

WEBER (1786–1826)

Carl Maria von Weber made a rather larger contribution

to German opera than Beethoven, and is blamed by many for paving the way for Wagner. The operas the bluffer is most likely to encounter are *Der Freischütz* (1821), a tale of foresters shooting things in the wood that is probably not ideal for those liable to leap out of their seats at the sound of gunshots; and *Euryanthe* (1823).

MEYERBEER (1791–1864)

Giacomo Meyerbeer was actually a Prussian-born Berliner called Jacob Liebmann Beer, but clearly felt that the adoption of an Italian first name might enhance his credibility as an opera composer. And it surely succeeded beyond his wildest dreams, because he became staggeringly successful as one of the first exponents of truly grand opera with the likes of *Robert le Diable* (1831) and *Les Huguenots* (1836). A true superstar of the mid-19th century, his reputation suffered after his death because he was rubbished by Wagner. His work was also suppressed by the Nazis because Meyerbeer was a Jew. The sheer grandeur of his operas makes it hard to get productions past the bean counters in most opera companies nowadays.

ROSSINI (1792–1868)

Gioachino Rossini was the most popular opera composer of his day, banging out no fewer than 39 of them before happily embarking on a near 40-year retirement in 1829. Given this high level of concentrated productivity, it should be no surprise that he frequently recycled his own music:

the overture of *Il Barbiere di Siviglia* (1816) was reputedly attached to three other operas before finding its final home. The *opera buffe* about the barber Figaro and *La Cenerentola* (1817), an easily digested version of the Cinderella story, are mainstays of the standard operatic repertoire. Among his other comedies, *L'italiana in Algeri* (1813) and the nicely reciprocal *Il Turco in Italia* (1814) get an occasional airing and the bluffer should approach them with the caution recommended for all operatic works making mention of North Africa or the Middle East. *Matilde di Shabran* (1821), staged by the Royal Opera in 2008, features an antisocial leading character, Corradino, whose misogynistic attitudes bore such a marked resemblance to those of one particular member of the audience that the 'happy ending' moved him to propose to his lady companion after the show. Worse still, she accepted. All bluffers should regard this as a terrible warning of the unexpected power of even second-rate opera.

Few of Rossini's many historical works make it to the stage nowadays. But the failure of the stage effects for the parting of the Red Sea in *Mosè in Egitto* (1818) was apparently a reliable source of hilarity in the composer's own day, and the bluffer should clearly seek out any revival in the hope of similar pleasure. Rossini's swansong, the epic *Guillaume Tell* (1829) is also well worth catching, at least by those who have the strength of character not to yell 'Hi ho, Silver!' during the overture.

BELLINI (1801–35)

Even before he achieved immortality as a cocktail, Vincenzo Bellini had staked a strong claim to that status with *Norma* (1831) and particularly with its great *soprano* aria 'Casta Diva'. The eponymous Druid priestess ends the piece clambering on to a funeral pyre with her lover: a fact for every bluffer's shortlist of dramatic operatic exits. Bellini's *I Capuleti e I Montecchi* (1830), unsurprisingly a version of *Romeo and Juliet*, and *I Puritani* (1835), an unlikely tale of the English Civil War based on Sir Walter Scott's *Old Mortality*, may also be encountered in performance from time to time. The latter should be cherished for its happy ending, made possible by a pardon for the Royalists from that well-known sentimental softie Oliver Cromwell.

DONIZETTI (1797–1848)

Gaetano Donizetti is known, like the -inis Ross and Bell, as a composer of *bel canto* opera. The bluffer will always do well to throw this term in, without having a clue what it means. Even those who have been to hundreds of operas and read extensively on the subject may well find that it still makes their heads swim. Literally, *bel canto* just means 'beautiful singing', which the bluffer might reasonably assume to be the objective of any opera before about the middle of the last century.

Donizetti composed around 75 operas, all tuneful in a rumty-tumty sort of way, and many bluffers will be able to get away with the simple verdict of an enthusiastic programme seller at the Buxton Festival many years ago: 'You can't go wrong with Donizetti!' Those most regularly performed are the comedies *L'elisir d'amore* (1832), oddly enough about an elixir of love, and *Don Pasquale* (1843), a moral tale about the folly of marrying in old age which every bluffer should inwardly digest. But Donizetti also wrote a huge number of historical dramas, including some based on British history, including *Anna Bolena* (1830) and *Maria Stuarda* (1835). In *Lucia di Lammermoor* (1835), based on a novel by Sir Walter Scott, Donizetti created the most famous mad scene in the whole of operatic history. Towards the end of his life, Donizetti himself went mad. As the Americans say: 'go figure'.

BERLIOZ (1803–69)

Hector Berlioz is best known as a French orchestral composer, but bluffers should be aware that he also wrote a few operas, of which the greatest is the massive *Les Troyens* (1863), with a *libretto* written by the composer himself, based on Virgil's *Aeneid*. Berlioz could not find anyone prepared to stage the full five-and-a-half-hour epic in his lifetime, but the traditional wooden horse has graced quite a few stages in more recent times.

GOUNOD (1818–93)

Charles Gounod wrote more than a dozen operas, of which only *Faust* (1859) has shown real staying power. Although a flop when first performed, it became a huge hit when revived in his home town of Paris in 1862 and was one of the most frequently performed operas in the world for the best part of a century, before falling from critical favour. But with big tunes, dancing and the perfect excuse for some gratuitous Walpurgisnacht spring festival nudity (in the hands of a literally minded director), there is little for the bluffer to dislike. And when you're explaining precisely why you don't dislike his work, you might drop into conversation that he lived in Blackheath, south London, for four years in his early 50s.

DELIBES (1836–91)

Léo Delibes was another French composer, best known for his ballets, who hit the operatic pop jackpot thanks to British Airways's hijacking of the 'Flower Duet' from *Lakmé* (1883) as its theme tune a century later. Lakmé is a Hindu priestess in India under the British Raj but no aircraft are involved in the story, so it cannot be the difficulty of fitting an Airbus on stage that makes performances such a rarity.

BORODIN (1833–87)

The Russian Romantic composer Alexander Borodin laboured for 18 years on his great historical opera *Prince Igor* (1890) but still did not manage to finish it, leaving that to Rimsky-Korsakov (*see* 'Supporting Chorus: The Also-Rans', page 67) and Glazunov after his death. Many bluffers will recognise the big tune from the Polovtsian dances because of its recycling in the 1953 musical *Kismet* as 'Stranger in Paradise' (the first line of which, as every schoolboy should know, is really 'Hold my hand, I'm a strange-looking parasite').

MUSSORGSKY (1839–81)

Borodin's friend and contemporary, Modest Mussorgsky provides the bluffer with a unique opportunity to recycle Winston Churchill's joke about Clement Attlee having 'much to be modest about'. A world-class alcoholic, Mussorgsky nevertheless completed the historical opera *Boris Godunov* (1873), which both Rimsky-Korsakov and Shostakovich felt the urge to improve. Rimsky-Korsakov also completed *Khovanschina* (1886), which Shostakovich again comprehensively revised, to bring it more in line with Mussorgsky's original modest intentions.

TCHAIKOVSKY (1840–93)

Pyotr Ilyich Tchaikovsky wrote ten operas, two of which have entered the world's operatic mainstream: *Eugene Onegin* (1879) and *The Queen of Spades* (1890), both based on Pushkin poems. The more frequently performed *Eugene Onegin* is the story of a villain who spurns the love of a country girl called Tatiana who has written to him setting out her feelings, then, for good measure, kills the fiancé of Tatiana's sister in a duel. Years later he pitches up in Moscow, finds Tatiana married to an elderly prince, and realises that she is stunningly beautiful and that he really loved her all along. He writes her a letter to that effect and she tells him to go and boil his head, so it has an unexpectedly happy ending. In the 'life imitating art' department, Pushkin was killed in a duel while Tchaikovsky was so keen to avoid becoming another Onegin that when one of his pupils at the Moscow Conservatory wrote to tell of her love for him, he married her, temporarily losing sight of the fact that he was homosexual. The marriage was about as successful as Onegin's belated attempt to woo Tatiana.

RIMSKY-KORSAKOV (1844–1908)

Nikolai Rimsky-Korsakov is best known as the composer of 'The Flight of the Bumble Bee' and for having a surname that sounds amusingly like 'Rip ze corsets off'. But he also wrote 15 operas of his own in addition to trying to make sense of those left by his modest friend Mussorgsky. They are all very Russian and most frequently performed there, but should not be shunned if found on offer elsewhere. *The Legend of the Invisible City of Kitezh and the Maiden Fevroniya* (1907) is a particular favourite, not least for the baroque splendour of its title.

BIZET (1838–75)

Georges Bizet wrote 15-or-so operas, but it was the last, *Carmen* (1875), that secured his place in history as the author of one of the most popular and successful operas ever written. Sadly this was not evident to the French composer himself, who died three months after its premiere, aged only 36, convinced by the critics that he had delivered 'a definite and hopeless flop'. Characteristically, no sooner was he dead than those same commentators announced that it was, in fact, a masterpiece. The other Bizet opera of which every bluffer should be aware is *The Pearl Fishers* (1863), a refreshingly short piece set in ancient Ceylon and including early on the memorable duet 'Au Fond du Temple Saint' sung by the pearl fishers Zurga and Nadir: a sort of 'Flower Duet' for blokes. Other Bizet works like *La Jolie Fille de Perth* (The Fair Maid of Perth) are unlikely to be encountered in performance outside the fair city from which it takes its name.

MASSENET (1842–1912)

Jules Massenet was the dominant figure in French opera for more than 30 years in the later 19th century. Of his 34 operas, *Manon* (1884) and *Werther* (1892) have remained staples of the repertory, though others are now staged after the obligatory lull during which he was considered to be a bit naff. Puccini considerately tacked a surname (Lescaut) on to his version of the Manon story to avoid needless confusion, though the bluffer should still check. Perhaps allowing the box office the pleasure of repeating the Met in New York's famous line when asked about a performance of *Manon*: 'That's Massenet, right?' 'No, sir, it's an evening performance.'

HUMPERDINCK (1854–1921)

Thinking of the elderly Anglo-Indian pop singer Gerry Dorsey when hearing the name of Engelbert Humperdinck is a solecism of which no bluffer should be guilty. Although he wrote other operas, the German composer's reputation rests entirely on *Hänsel und Gretel*

(1893), the classic tale of babes in the wood. Much as the singer's rests entirely on 'Please Release Me'.

LEONCAVALLO (1858–1919)

Ruggiero Leoncavallo is also marked down as a one-hit wonder, thanks to his first opera *Pagliacci* (1892), a two-act, one-hour melodrama that concludes with multiple stabbings and the memorable closing line 'La commedia è finitta' (now out of copyright and ideal for a tombstone). He wrote several others, including *La Bohème* (1897), and was tremendously unlucky that Puccini sneaked in with a work on the same subject the year before.

MASCAGNI (1863–1945)

Pietro Mascagni wrote 15 operas but is also known for only one, *Cavalleria Rusticana* (1890), a jolly hour of seduction and murder in a Sicilian village, accompanied by ravishing tunes ('Intermezzo', particularly, brought to the masses courtesy of the film *Raging Bull* and an advert for Kleenex). Because of their compatible lengths, dates of composition, subject matter and popular appeal, *Cavelleria Rusticana* often features in a double bill with *Pagliacci: Cav & Pag*, to which the true bluffer will knowingly add 'by Masc and Leon'.

DEBUSSY (1862–1918)

Claude Debussy is famed as the composer of the operatic one-off *Pelléas et Mélisande* (1902), which is universally agreed to be a landmark in 20th-century music, albeit a landmark no one has subsequently chosen to revisit. Nothing much happens for five musically continuous acts. The Glyndebourne production of 1999 attempted to break the mould by opening with Mélisande naked, but failed to live up to its early promise.

SMETANA (1824–84)

Bedrich Smetana is a Czech composer of nine operas, best known for *The Bartered Bride* (1866) – not to be confused with that old Scottish culinary favourite, the battered bridie – a nutritious meat pastry. With a drinking song, a visiting circus and a happy ending, it has much to commend it for an uplifting and intellectually undemanding night out.

DVORÁK (1841–1904)

Although best known in the UK for orchestrating Hovis commercials, the Czech Antonín Dvořák also wrote a number of operas, of which one, *Rusalka* (1901), has achieved a permanent place in the international operatic repertoire. The story of a water nymph who famously sings a song to the moon, the combination of the words 'water', 'nymph' and 'moon' often tempts opera houses to adorn posters for *Rusalka* with images of attractive naked ladies. The bluffer who is tempted by these would do better to invest his money at Spearmint Rhino.

JANÁCEK (1854–1928)

Completing our Czech threesome, Leoš Janáček wrote nine operas. *Jenufa* (1904) and *Kát'a Kabanová* (1921) feature miserable eastern Europeans who at least have the consolation of a handy river in which to drown themselves or their offspring. *The Cunning Little Vixen* (1924) may not be the only opera in which the lead *soprano* gets shot, but is certainly unique in requiring her to dress up as a fox beforehand and have her fur removed afterwards. *The Makropulos Case* (1926) is about a 340-year-old woman who unsurprisingly dies of natural causes. Many well-informed observers consider that the power of Janáček's music more than compensates for his grim subject matter, but the bluffer should be under no illusions that he is in for a jolly night out.

STRAUSS (1864–1949)

Richard Strauss was a prolific German composer of operas. His early efforts, *Salome* (1905) and *Elektra* (1909), have made Strauss enduringly popular with orchestral musicians, partly because of the opulent sounds they are invited to produce, but mainly because they are the shortest one-act operas regularly performed on their own, rather than as half of a double bill. *Der Rosenkavalier* (1911) makes up for these by lasting three-and-a-half hours, but compensates by offering many ravishing melodies, including waltzes more in the style of Johann Strauss (no relation). This is the most accessible of Strauss's work for the bluffer who does not rate brevity above all. Other Strauss operas that are likely to be encountered include *Die Frau Ohne Schatten* (1919), which is about a woman without a shadow, *Intermezzo* (1924), *Arabella* (1933), *Die Schweigsame Frau* (The Silent Woman, 1935) which is noisier than one might expect, *Daphne* (1938) and *Capriccio* (1942), which had its premiere in Munich despite the inconvenience of nightly Allied air raids. Taken together, it is hard to dispute that this body of work entitles Strauss to be considered the greatest of 20th-century opera composers.

RAVEL (1875–1937)

Maurice Ravel wrote two frequently paired short operas, *L'Heure Espagnole* (1911) and *L'Enfant et Les Sortilèges* (1925). The first concerns an absent-minded Spanish clockmaker, the second a rude child who gets his comeuppance when the inanimate objects in his room come to life, followed by some implausibly anthropomorphic plants and animals outside. The best news for the bluffer is that *L'Heure* is over in a mere 50 minutes.

BERG (1885–1935)

Alban Berg is an Austrian composer, noted for *Wozzeck* (1925) and *Lulu* (1937). The bluffer should be aware that the key words normally attached to Berg's music are 'atonal' and 'avant garde'. Under no circumstances should you attend a performance of *Lulu* expecting to enjoy a performance by the diminutive Scottish songstress of the same name, and to come out humming the tunes. On the other hand *Lulu* does progress from gold-digging infidelity to death at the hands of Jack the Ripper via murder, blackmail and prostitution, so dull it isn't.

WEILL (1900–50)

A refugee from Nazi Germany, Kurt Weill is best known as the composer of *The Threepenny Opera* (1933) which, confusingly, isn't an opera at all, but a musical. Weill's authentic operas include *The Rise and Fall of the City of Mahagonny* (1930), which bluffers should know is a fable about lumberjacks and whores set in America and has nothing to do with the tropical hardwood popular in traditional English furniture. It also features a tenor character called Fatty, displaying either a marked lack of imagination or an acceptance of the reality of typical singers' physiques between the wars. The other Weill opera most likely to be encountered is *Street Scene* (1946), in which the street in question is in New York.

GERSHWIN (1898–1937)

George Gershwin is, like Weill, better known as a composer of musicals (and 'Rhapsody in Blue') but gave the world one undisputed opera, *Porgy and Bess* (1935), an American classic set in Catfish Row, Charleston, South Carolina. With songs including 'Summertime', 'It Ain't Necessarily So' and 'I Got Plenty o' Nuttin', there is every chance that bluffers will leave humming the tunes and wondering whether they have really witnessed an opera at all.

PROKOFIEV (1891–1953)

Sergei Prokofiev will undoubtedly be better known to you as the composer of the ballet score *Romeo and Juliet*, but he also wrote as many as nine operas of which the most frequently performed are *The Love for Three Oranges* (1921), a satirical work that mainly concerns animated playing cards rather than a fruit machine, and *The Fiery Angel* (1955). The epic *War and Peace* (1946) also merits the bluffer's attention for its sheer scale; its recreation of the battle of Borodino is thought to have set a record for the number of performers observed on the stage of the ROH – one which seems unlikely to be beaten in a hurry.

STRAVINSKY (1882–1971)

Igor Stravinsky wrote at least seven operas we know about, of which the most frequently performed is *The Rake's Progress* (1951). Set in London and inspired by William Hogarth's prints, with a *libretto* by W.H. Auden and Chester Kallman, it has claims to be the quintessential English opera – particularly when seen in the classic and frequently revived 1975 Glyndebourne production, with designs by David Hockney. Which is odd when one considers that the cosmopolitan Stravinsky lived pretty much everywhere else, progressing through Russian, French and US citizenship before being buried in Venice.

SHOSTAKOVICH (1906–75)

Dmitri Shostakovich started his operatic career with *The Nose* (1930), surely the only opera to offer a tenor a role as a human proboscis, and reached his peak with *Lady Macbeth of Mtensk* (1934), a masterpiece of Slav misery clearly influenced by Janáček, since the title character ends up in an icy river.

VAUGHAN WILLIAMS (1872–1958)

Making a late entrance stage left, the Brits finally reappeared on the operatic scene for the first time since Purcell. They were led by Ralph Vaughan Williams who, despite his Welsh-sounding name, was actually born in the Cotswolds and related to both Charles Darwin and Josiah Wedgwood (useful bluffing points). He wrote five operas which are probably fairly characterised as being of specialist interest rather than mainstream. Nevertheless, the bluffer may wish to catch the one-act *Riders to the Sea* (1937) and the full-scale *Sir John in Love* (1929), which covers the same ground as Verdi's *Falstaff,* but in English folk melodies rather than Italian grandeur.

BRITTEN (1913–76)

Benjamin Britten wrote 15 operas, from *Paul Bunyan* (1941) to *Death in Venice* (1973). The bluffer should at least be familiar with *Peter Grimes* (1945), *Albert Herring* (1947), *Billy Budd* (1951), *The Turn of the Screw* (1954) and *A Midsummer Night's Dream* (1960), all of which are regularly produced and make Britten the most performed composer of operas to have been born in the 20th century. Britten operas tend to contain a large dollop of repressed homosexual desire and their lead character often bears an uncanny resemblance to Britten's partner, the tenor Peter Pears. No bluffer, though, should underestimate the power of the music: drowning is too good for any member of the audience who considers it all right to talk through the sea interludes in *Peter Grimes* because no one is actually on stage singing at them while they are being played.

TIPPETT (1905–98)

Michael Tippett wrote six operas, which the bluffer is safe to say are not as tuneful or accessible as those of his near contemporary and compatriot Britten. *The Midsummer Marriage* (1955), *King Priam* (1962) and *The Knot Garden* (1970) may all be encountered in performance, though nothing like as frequently as they no doubt will be in the second half of the 21st century when Tippett is inevitably rediscovered as an overlooked genius.

RECITATIVE: CLASSIC OPERA PLOTS AND TUNES

THE PLOTS

The ultimate opera plot centres on a pretty (and, in past times, probably rather plump) young woman who is gravely impoverished and/or suffering from a terminal illness. A man is madly in love with her but cannot hope to win her heart because she is:

a) already madly in love with someone else; and/or
b) from a vastly different social class; and/or
c) already betrothed to an elderly guardian; and/or
d) incredibly frigid; or
e) a nun; or
f) a lesbian (20th century and later operas only); or
g) a bloke in drag.

The librettist then throws in a few more characters, at least two of whom will be operating under a false identity, for reasons too complex to grasp until at least your third reading of the synopsis. All of these will be in love with at least one of the principals, and possibly both of them.

In a classic opera, you may assume with a reasonable degree of assurance that Character A will be in love with Character B, who will be in love with Character C, who will in turn be in love with Character A. Or, if the librettist was aiming for something a bit out of the ordinary, Character D, E or F.

You can also be more or less certain that anyone presenting themselves as a slave or a prisoner of war is, in fact, concealing his or her identity as a member of some royal family or other.

To take an example, Handel's opera *Partenope* concerns, unsurprisingly, (A) Partenope, Queen of Naples (a *soprano*; *see* 'Glossary', page 117) who is being pursued by four suitors: (B) Arsace, Prince of Corinth (originally a *castrato*); (C) Armindo, Prince of Rhodes (a *contralto* dressed as a man); (D) Emilio, Prince of Cumae (a tenor); and (E) Euremine (a *contralto* or *mezzo-soprano* who is not merely another woman dressed as a man, but really *is* a woman called Rosmira in disguise). You will note how the librettist has cunningly added to the confusion by endowing at least two of the protagonists with reasonably similar names. A is in love with B, who was formerly betrothed to E. B, who has the good fortune to be marginally more intelligent than the sisters in *Così fan Tutte*, has seen through E's disguise and knows that he is really a she. A rejects a proposal of marriage from D, who then declares war on her (as you do) but is defeated and captured by B, though E successfully claims the credit for the victory. C is spurned by A. E challenges B to a duel, which B accepts – but racily insists that they must fight bare-chested, which thoroughly puts the mockers on E's disguise. B and E are then reconciled, and A gets together with C, presumably leaving D grumbling like Muttley the dog.

And if you think that is confusing, it was only chosen because it seemed like one of Handel's simpler operas.

In 18th-century *opera seria* and later grand opera, the impoverished/terminally ill woman at the centre of the plot will die, noisily, possibly along with several other members of the cast. In extreme cases, some members of the orchestra may elect to take the easy way out too.

In *opera buffa* and later comic opera, the problems will be miraculously resolved and everyone will live happily ever after.

The former is clearly a much more realistic take on how life tends to work out in practice.

Opera plots may be more minutely characterised as follows:

He loves her but it's complicated, then she dies

The simplest model, it has worked for such enduring favourites as *Carmen, Dido and Aeneas, La Traviata, La Bohème* and *Manon/Manon Lescaut*. *Orfeo ed Euridice* offers the unexpected and frankly implausible twist that she dies, but is then restored to life.

He loves her but it's complicated, then he dies

The story of *Werther*, in which the eponymous hero shoots himself on account of unrequited love, but with such poor aim that he takes a full act to die.

She loves him but it's complicated, then she dies

The basic premise of *Rigoletto* and *Madama Butterfly*, in which the leading lady falls for a worthless anti-hero (The Duke, Pinkerton).

They love each other but it's complicated, then they both die

This covers a surprisingly broad range from *Aida* to *Tristan und Isolde* by way of, for example, *Otello*, *The Snow Maiden* and *Theodora*.

He loves her even though she is a monumentally deranged and cruel mass murderer, and the audience is expected to believe that they live happily ever after

That would be *Turandot*, in a nutshell.

He loves her but has to use all his ingenuity to get past her elderly guardian; they then live happily ever after...or at any rate until the next opera in the series

Il Barbiere di Siviglia, before it all goes wrong for Count and Countess Almaviva in *The Marriage of Figaro*.

He sleeps around and then dies, and serves him right

The essence of *Don Giovanni*.

They are unfaithful to their fiancés because they can't see through the simplest of disguises, yet everything works out eventually

The hugely implausible premise of *Così fan Tutte*.

It's all really about Freemasonry, you know

All any bluffer need ever grasp about *The Magic Flute*.

A dwarf steals a ring with apocalyptic consequences

Fifteen hours of Wagner's *Der Ring des Nibelugen* summarised in eight words.

WAYS TO GO: DEATH IN OPERA

There are almost as many ways to die in opera as there are in real life, where, as anyone who has studied London's Bills of Mortality from 1629 to 1836 will know, the scope for human ingenuity is almost infinite.

Puccini clearly realised that he wasn't really trying when he had his early heroine dying of thirst in a desert (*Manon Lescaut*) or expiring from tuberculosis (*La Bohème*). In *Tosca,* he has the eponymous heroine leaping from the battlements of Rome's Castel Sant'Angelo. After concerted action by the National Amalgamated Union of Sopranos & Allied Trades, Etc. (NAUSEATE), theatre managements were persuaded to provide inflated cushions to break her fall, which created the always entertaining possibility that *Tosca* might bounce back into view after her dramatic exit. Sadly, this is a much less regular event since the traditional pie-eating *soprano* was replaced with a slender one who clearly spends her nights off at a Weight Watchers group.

The concept of the leaping *soprano* had already been established with Senta in Wagner's *Der Fliegende Holländer*, who jumps to her death off a cliff. The heroines of *The Queen of Spades, Kát'a Kabanová* and *Lady Macbeth of Mtensk* end it all in rivers.

Sharp instruments obviously impose fewer pressures on the director and props department: Cio-Cio-San in *Madama Butterfly* commits hara-kiri; the sorely provoked Don José stabs Carmen; and Jack the Ripper accounts for Berg's Lulu.

Then there is poison: Lakmé eats a poisonous datura leaf; Francesco Cilea's Adriana Lecouvreur kisses a poisoned bunch of violets; and Selika in Meyerbeer's *L'Africaine* inhales the poisonous fumes of a mançanilla tree (which has not, in practice, ever killed anyone else).

However, all these seem like amateur efforts compared with some of the unlikely *soprano* exits available. Aida is buried alive with Radamès and Norma is immolated on a pyre, while Rimsky-Korsakov's Snow Maiden simply melts in the sunshine. Elektra dances herself to death. Niobe in Agostino Steffani's *Niobe, Regina di Tiebe* turns to stone in despair after witnessing all her children burned to death in a conflagration, and her husband committing suicide as a result.

Rachel in Fromental Halévy's *La Juive* hurls herself into a cauldron of burning oil; Alfredo Catalini's aptly named Wally throws herself into a passing Alpine avalanche; while Fenella, the dumb girl of Daniel Auber's *La Muette di Portici* (also known as *Masaniello*) hands in her dinner pail in a stream of burning lava during an eruption of

Mount Vesuvius. Though all are surely capped by Francis Poulenc's *Dialogues of the Carmelites*, in which an entire convent of nuns is guillotined. You may have noted that all the operas in this paragraph are thoroughly obscure; strangely enough, few opera houses ever seem inspired to rise to the challenge of trying to stage them.

As a general rule, heroines rarely die of extreme old age, though that is the fate of Janáček's Elina Makropulos. And many a bluffer will surely wish that more *soprano*s would follow the fine example of Antonia in Jacques Offenbach's *Tales of Hoffman*, who simply sings herself to death.

It's not just *soprano*s who face death on stage: Scarpia is stabbed by Tosca, Otello stabs himself, Peter Grimes and Wozzeck drown. Cavarodossi is shot by firing squad in *Tosca*, Billy Budd is hanged. On a larger scale, there is an *auto-da-fé* (mass burning of heretics) in Verdi's *Don Carlos*, while the entire community of old believers walk into a pyre together in Mussorgsky's *Khovanschina*, and the whole shooting match of Valhalla goes up in flames at the conclusion of *Götterdamerüng*. It is not considered appropriate to look at one's watch as the curtain comes down and say 'About [expletive deleted] time, too.'

NAME THAT TUNE

There are a handful of big tunes that every bluffer should be able to recognise and, ideally, hum to demonstrate their devotion to opera. The list that follows should not include 'Just One Cornetto' ('O Sole Mio') which sounds as though it might well come from an opera, but does not.

Aria	What to say	What not to say
Au Fond du Temple Saint (The Pearl Fishers)	Two blokes vowing eternal friendship despite both fancying the same girl: what could possibly go wrong?	That hot threesome in Act 2 is one of my all-time favourites.
Casta Diva (Norma)	Do you prefer the classic versions by Maria Callas (p. 98) or Joan Sutherland? (p. 98)	I'd like to cast a diva myself. Preferably from the top of the stage rigging.
Che Faro Senza Euridice (Orfeo ed Euridice)	What could be lovelier than Kathleen Ferrier (p. 97) singing 'What is Life Without Thee?'	Oh no, you haven't! She's behind you!
Che Gelida Manina (La Bohème)	Her tiny hand is frozen.	My dad told me you should always go for birds with small hands.
Der Hölle Rache (The Magic Flute)	I can never quite believe that The Queen of the Night will hit those amazing notes.	Ditch the princess, mate, and go for her mother.
Flower Duet (Lakmé)	I'd really love to see a production of Lakmé.	Say what you like about British Airways, at least they're not Ryanair.
La Donna è Mobile (Rigoletto)	That duke, eh? He can hardly talk about fidelity.	Fancy being able to order a kebab on a smartphone in those days.
Largo al Factotum (Il Barbiere di Siviglia)	It's truly amazing that he can sing those words so fast.	So how long is it till he gets married?
Nessun Dorma (Turandot)	How could Calaf love a monster like Turandot?	Why are England still so rubbish at taking penalties?

Aria	What to say	What not to say
O Mio Babbino Caro (*Gianni Schicchi*)	So moving that she sings this to her father right in the middle of that awful family feud.	What a load of fuss about a flipping monkey.
Pur ti Miro (*L'Incoronazione di Poppea*)	Why do the most ghastly characters get the most divine music?	Anyone fancy a pint?
Un Bel Dì (*Madama Butterfly*)	One beautiful day he will come back to her.	Oh good, I love a happy ending.
Va, Pensiero (*Nabucco*)	The chorus of the Hebrew slaves will always have a special place in my heart.	Why are they asking those poor pensioners to clear off?
The Ride of the Valkyries (*Die Walküre*)	I shall never regret the time I have invested in getting to know Wagner.	Who wrote the music for *Apocalypse Now* again?
Vedi! Le Fosche Notturne (*Il Trovatore*)	A fine rendition of the anvil chorus.	Just the sort of noisy carry on you'd expect from a bunch of gypsies.
Votre Toast, Je Peux Vous le Rendre (*Carmen*)	Cigarettes and bullfighting: has there ever been a more non-PC opera, Tristram?	What d'you mean 'I'm toast'?
When I am laid in Earth (*Dido and Aeneas*)	So very moving, Purcell.	The sooner she gets laid, the sooner we can go home.
William Tell Overture (*Guillaume Tell*)	Such a shame that Rossini's historical operas are so neglected.	Me Tonto, you Kemosabe.

ℬ

'My number one rule became "Don't f*** up the music." It's not the job of a set designer to make an opera come alive. That's the job of the composer, conductor, orchestra and singers.'

David Hockney

LONG INTERVAL: OPERA SUPPORTING CAST

What is needed to stage an opera? A composer and librettist, obviously. Some singers, an orchestra and a conductor. But left to themselves, they would be dough without yeast. The completed, delicious confection also requires the input of all those other people who wander on to take a bow on opening night, and the critics who tell us what to think of them.

THE DIRECTOR

The director can make all the difference between a magically memorable evening and three hours spent with one's eyes shut, wishing one had stayed at home and listened to the opera on CD.

Typically, the director will want to make his mark by challenging the audience's preconceptions. Setting the opera in the period that its date of composition and stage directions suggest is far too easy. Why not wrench it into another historical era entirely, even though the characters will still be singing words and behaving in ways that are clearly indicative of a period when very different social norms prevailed?

Sometimes this works well: ENO in London has a classic production of *Rigoletto* by Jonathan Miller, successfully updated to the 1930s. On the other hand, the same company once laid on an altogether less cherishable production of *Carmen* set in a scrapyard full of American limousines ('Car men', geddit?) and the 'iconoclastic' Calixto Bieito take on *A Masked Ball,* featuring lavatories and male rape.

Audiences, who are naturally much more simple-minded than directors, tend to vote with their wallets for productions that they find comfortable and enjoyable. So the *Tosca* devised and designed by Franco Zeffirelli for the Royal Opera ran for more than 240 performances over 40 years from 1964 to 2004, when the sets and costumes were sold to Lyric Opera of Chicago. By contrast, the Royal Opera's 1991 production of *Les Huguenots,* bafflingly incorporating imagery of the Berlin Wall and a pool full of bathing beauties, saw just one short run before being unceremoniously scrapped.

THE DESIGNERS

The designers work with the director to create the sets and costumes that can either have an audience burst into spontaneous applause when the curtain goes up (as often happened at the start of the second act of the Royal Opera's 1984 production of *Der Rosenkavalier*) or sink into quiet despair. Typically there will be a set designer, costume designer and lighting designer. Occasionally, as with the multi-talented Franco Zeffirelli, they will all be the same person.

David Hockney, who designed both sets and costumes for Glyndebourne's *The Rake's Progress* in 1975, shared an important lesson for all designers in a *Guardian* interview in 2010: 'My number one rule became "Don't f*** up the music." It's not the job of a set designer to make an opera come alive. That's the job of the composer, conductor, orchestra and singers.'

Audiences tend to vote with their wallets for productions that they find comfortable and enjoyable.

One designer who inadvertently flouted this rule was the Brit Roger Butlin, whose 2012 obituaries devoted less space to his many triumphs than to the 1979 Wexford production of Spontini's *La Vestale*, in which the steeply raked set required a coating of sticky lemonade to enable the cast to keep their feet. Sadly, this offended one Irish stagehand, who did such a marvellous job of washing it off, according to contemporary accounts, that the singers all ended up in a struggling heap on the edge of the orchestra pit, reducing the audience to helpless laughter.

Wiseacres will boringly assure you that nearly all such stories of great operatic disasters are completely apocryphal, but this Wexford incident is well attested, and you may download a podcast of the BBC's *Desert Island Discs* from 1982 in which the legendary British *soprano* Dame Eva Turner (to many, the greatest Turandot of all) informs Roy Plomley that she did indeed leap from the battlements at the end of *Tosca* only to bounce straight back into the view of the audience; something which you will be told a thousand times 'never happened'. Similarly, the Austrian tenor Leo Slezak swore that a stagehand once made too early a start in hauling off the swan-powered boat on which he was to make his exit in Wagner's *Lohengrin*, enabling him to utter the immortal ad lib, 'What time's the next swan?'

THE CHORUS

The chorus comprises 40 to 80 assorted *sopranos*, *mezzo-sopranos*, tenors and basses of all ages and shapes. The younger and prettier ones are probably aspiring stars who are just waiting for one of the principals to break a leg (and may have a supply of marbles in their pocket to increase the chances of this happening) so that they may receive the *42nd Street*-style call: 'You're going to have to go on and save the show!' The older and lumpier ones are just regular guys who enjoy singing and acting in a group at terrible hours for even worse money, and usually really like a drink.

THE CHORUS MASTER

This is the dinner-jacketed figure who pitches up at curtain calls in the middle of the chorus, and tries to take all the credit for its contribution to the performance. No bluffer should ever betray ignorance by muttering 'Who the hell's that?' Now that the animal rights movement has done away with the lion tamer and that bloke who used to teach seals to play a simple tune on motor horns, the chorus master stands alone as the last surviving example of someone who is prepared to risk everything to subdue a bunch of living creatures and persuade them to sing in tune.

THE ACTOR

The actor is the person who is up on stage but doesn't appear to be singing. Unless it is a stagehand who has just fallen from the ceiling and is suffering from concussion, waiting for the stretcher-bearers to arrive. Actors tend to be employed to pad out large productions and do things that the chorus are too busy, too unattractive or too bolshy to do themselves, such as standing around stark naked in the name of art.

THE PROMPTER

In the bluffer's vision of opera, there will be a small box towards the front of the stage where a prompter sits with a copy of the *libretto*, ready to yell out any forgotten line. In practice this rarely happens, except once memorably at a performance by the Bolshoi Opera where every single line of an exceptionally long Russian epic was loudly yelled from the side of the stage just before the singers started up.

THE STAGEHAND

The stagehand opens and closes the curtains and moves the scenery around, these days often with the help of computerised mechanical aids. Older bluffers yearn for the days when scenery used to be wheeled about by ill-concealed workmen, hoping that some hilarious mishap might cause the evening to degenerate into a *Morecambe & Wise* sketch.

THE ADMINISTRATOR

The main qualifications for a successful career as an opera administrator are the possession of a dinner jacket, a lugubrious face and the ability not to burst into tears when an audience sighs or boos. This is because the administrator's principal public role is to appear before the curtains at the start of a performance to announce that the *soprano* or tenor for whom the audience has saved their money and travelled many miles to hear is indisposed. Or, perhaps worse, too ill to sing properly but gamely battling on and 'craving the indulgence' of the assembled ticket-holders. As a general rule, the appearance of anyone in a dinner jacket on stage before the curtain goes up is about as welcome in an opera house as the arrival of a practical joker dressed as the Grim Reaper in a twilight home.

THE CRITIC

Critics are not like other people. As evidence of this, witness the behaviour of one hatchet-faced old brute observed at the Wexford Festival over several years. The story goes that she religiously sat through every performance, including the 'Operatic Scenes' designed to provide a showcase for talented younger performers, yet she never clapped, cracked a smile or gave any other indication that she might be enjoying herself in the slightest. The penny finally dropped after overhearing her breakfast conversation with a bearded drip who similarly seemed to be having the worst holiday of his life: they were both critics (albeit critics for publications so specialised that they were almost certainly read only by other critics). The bluffer should be aware that it is considered very bad form indeed for a critic to betray his or her feelings by actually appearing to enjoy a show.

But then everyone should be able to work that out from the fact that almost every opera review is a litany of the ways in which the performers, players, director and designer have fallen short of the idealised conception of the work that the critic carries around in his or her bulging cranium. Which is perhaps fair enough, given that the job title is 'critic' not 'cheerleader'.

As a general rule, it is safe to look forward keenly to operas that have been comprehensively slated by the critics; they are rarely, if ever, nearly as bad as the reviews suggest. The rare production that attracts a five-star 'rave', on the other hand, almost invariably fails to live up to its ecstatic billing and the unrealistically high expectations that this has raised.

Popular singers whose repertoires include a few operatic arias and who are therefore regularly described in the tabloid press as 'opera stars'...should not be confused with 'genuine opera singers'.

GOLDEN VOCAL CORDS: GREAT OPERA PERFORMERS

Was it all better in the old days? The debate about whether standards of opera singing have gone to hell in the proverbial handcart is a game of 'keepy-uppy' that opera aficionados are happy to play almost indefinitely. Luckily for the bluffer, it is impossible to provide a definitive answer because so many supposedly great performers expired before the invention of recording. And even that technological breakthrough is of limited assistance, given that the earliest recordings of legendary singers tend to be indistinguishable from those of a wasp in a jar, and even later 78rpm discs convey little sense of what once drove audiences to frenzied adulation.

Key names that the bluffer should recognise include:

Farinelli (1705–82)

Legendary Italian *castrato* and the subject of an entertaining but not necessarily entirely accurate biopic in 2004, which also made him out to be a legendary sexual athlete. The bluffer should be able to summarise in one word the two good reasons that make this seem highly unlikely.

Emanuel Schikaneder (1751–1812)

Singer, actor, dramatist and impresario who was not only the original Papageno in *The Magic Flute,* but also the author of its *libretto* and taught Mozart that he was missing a trick by not making the bird-catcher and his love Papagena stutter in their climactic duet. These are all handy facts to keep in mind for a pub quiz.

Jenny Lind (1820–87)

Soprano known as 'the Swedish nightingale' who achieved huge fame across Europe and America: retired from the operatic stage in 1849. Sadly unrecorded, but commemorated in a class of steam engines of the London, Brighton and South Coast Railway and in a type of soup.

Nellie Melba (1861–1931)

Australian *soprano*, a megastar in her day, who gave more farewell concerts than Frank Sinatra. Now remembered less for her performances than as a type of toast and a peach-based dessert, both created in her honour by the great French chef Auguste Escoffier who saw her in *Lohengrin* at the ROH in 1892. This sort of information could seriously enhance your bluffing credentials.

Enrico Caruso (1873–1921)
Legendary Italian tenor who was the first recording artist to sell more than a million copies of a record. Smoked two packets of Egyptian cigarettes a day and tragically died at the age of 48 in the finest opera tradition.

Feodor Chaliapin (1873–1938)
Russian contemporary of Caruso who is rated one of the greatest bass singers of all time. Also credited with introducing naturalistic acting to the operatic stage, as opposed to just standing there and belting it out.

Richard Tauber (1891–1948)
Austrian tenor who made his name in Mozart but later became more famous for his roles in operettas; a great favourite in Britain, where he lived from 1940.

Kathleen Ferrier (1912–53)
Much-loved British *contralto*, said at the time of her tragically early death to be the most famous woman in the country after the Queen – and certainly the most famous person of either sex ever to have lived in Silloth, west Cumbria. Her only operatic roles were in Britten's *The Rape of Lucretia* and Gluck's *Orfeo ed Euridice,* but she achieved immortality with her recordings of Orfeo's 'Che Farò' and the folk song 'Blow the Wind Southerly'.

Elisabeth Schwarzkopf (1915–2006)
Renowned German-born *soprano* who acquired British citizenship through marriage, but wisely refrained from anglicising her name to 'Blackhead'.

Maria Callas (1923–77)

American-born Greek *soprano* who initially won fame for her outstanding stage presence, combining a very distinctive voice with unusual physical acting prowess, but was latterly even better known as the mistress of the shipping magnate Aristotle Onassis until her position was usurped by Jacqueline Kennedy.

Dietrich Fischer-Diskau (1925–2012)

German baritone famed for his sublime voice and the breadth of his repertoire, extending far beyond the opera house (and not just to the pub opposite, as is the case with most musicians).

Joan Sutherland (1926–2010)

Australian *soprano* famous for going mad at the ROH as Lucia in 1959, and dubbed 'La Stupenda' in Venice in 1960. Known particularly for *bel canto* roles and unaccountably not commemorated in any dessert whatsoever.

Montserrat Caballé (1933–)

Garrulous and substantial Spanish *soprano* equally famous for her performances of *bel canto* roles and her 1988 duet with Freddie Mercury, 'Barcelona'. On one occasion she memorably provoked a cry of 'Get on with it!' from the audience (in *Il Viaggio a Reims* at Covent Garden, 1992).

Luciano Pavarotti (1935–2007)

Legendary Italian tenor renowned for his magnificent voice and, latterly, his almost equally magnificent corpulence. Dubbed 'the King of the High Cs' for his early performances of Donizetti's works, he became a renowned interpreter of the classic Verdi and Puccini tenor roles. Also famed far beyond the world's opera houses for his concert performances as one of The Three Tenors [*see* 'Plácido Domingo' and 'José Carreras' below], of which he constituted one-third by numbers and more than half by weight – though the true opera bluffer should never admit to having heard of The Three Tenors. Pavarotti latterly married a Mantovani, though not as a career move since she was unrelated to the popular purveyor of light classics.

Plácido Domingo (1941–)

Polymathic Spanish singer and conductor who has so far performed more than 140 operatic roles: having mastered just about all the decent tenor parts, he began singing baritone roles in 2009. Whether this will lead to a parallel concert career as one of The Three Baritones remains open to question.

Kiri Te Kanawa (1944–)

New Zealand *soprano* perhaps unfairly more famous for performing at the ill-fated marriage of Prince Charles and Lady Diana Spencer than for her many fine stage roles. The bluffer should be aware that her adoptive mother was distantly related to Sir Arthur Sullivan of Gibert and Sullivan fame: not a lot of people know that.

José Carreras (1946–)

Spanish tenor famed for his performances in Verdi

and Puccini, for being the smallest of The Three Tenors, and for surviving leukaemia against very lengthy odds.

Anne Sofie von Otter (1955–)

Swedish *mezzo-soprano* particularly noted for her trouser roles. Tragically the title role in Janáček's *The Cunning Little Vixen* calls for a full *soprano*, as who would not pay good money to see an otter playing a fox?

Bryn Terfel (1965–)

Popular Welsh bass-baritone whose real surname is Jones, as you might expect. The bluffer should also be aware that the single 'f' in Welsh is pronounced 'v'. Renowned particularly for his performances of Mozart and Wagner.

Angela Georghiu (1965–)

Romanian *soprano* renowned for her fine voice and diva-like ways. Married in 1996 to the French tenor Roberto Alagna (1963–), they together became known as 'opera's golden couple', particularly by themselves. They announced that they had split in 2009 but reunited in 2011 only to divorce in 2013.

Danielle de Niese (1979–)

Sri Lankan–Australian–American *soprano* who was so convincing as a sexy dancing Cleopatra in the 2005, 2006 and 2009 Glyndebourne productions of Handel's *Giulio Cesare* that she became the second wife of Glyndebourne chairman Gus Christie.

There are a number of popular singers whose repertoires include a few operatic arias and who are therefore regularly described in the tabloid press as 'opera stars': Katherine Jenkins (1980–) is a prime example. Bluffers should be aware that most so-called aficionados insist that these 'popular classical-crossover' artistes should not be confused with 'genuine opera singers', but feel free to enjoy yourself.

Why not have simpler plots in which A and B both love each other, get married and live happily ever after, without B dying of tuberculosis or being felled by a passing avalanche?

FINALE: OPERETTA, THE MUSICAL AND OPERA TODAY

OPERETTA

Opera began as the favoured entertainment of wealthy aristocrats. But by the middle of the 19th century, Europe had spawned a growing and prosperous middle class who liked the idea of a story told with some thumping good tunes, but lacked the colossal attention span, cast-iron buttocks and sheer delight in human misery demanded by conventional opera. Clearly it was the ideal time for a spot of commercially attractive dumbing down.

Why not have simpler plots in which A and B both love each other, get married and live happily ever after, without B dying of tuberculosis or being felled by a passing avalanche? Even better, why not move the creaking plot along with some simple and snappy spoken dialogue between the eagerly awaited tunes? From such heretical thinking sprang operetta or, as it would no doubt be called if invented today, Opera Lite.

Operetta emerged in Paris in the 1850s and its invention is credited to a French composer called **Hervé (1825–92)**: a good name for the bluffer to bandy around since no one else will ever have heard of him (but take care to avoid confusing him with the creator of *Tintin*, Hergé). However, the name that will naturally spring to the mind of non-bluffers as the first master of the genre is **Jacques Offenbach (1819–80)**. Like many great French composers before and no doubt since, Offenbach wasn't really French at all: he was a German, born Jakob Eberst, the son of a Jewish cantor in Cologne.

The French authorities were not at all keen to allow such lowbrow shenanigans as this new-fangled operetta in their capital's theatres, so Offenbach enterprisingly created a small theatre of his own, in which his first great success *Orphée aux Enfers* (Orpheus in the Underworld) was staged in 1858. There followed almost a hundred other light, witty and topical operettas, of which those with most enduring appeal have proved to be *La Belle Hélène* (1864) and *La Périchole* (1868).

Like the stand-up comedian who would much prefer to be playing *Hamlet*, Offenbach's real ambition was to write a proper opera and, touchingly enough, he did. But in true operatic tradition, he died before completing it, albeit from thoroughly unromantic heart failure occasioned by acute gout. *Les Contes d'Hoffmann* (The

Tales of Hoffmann) was first performed posthumously in 1881 and continues to feature in the operatic repertoire, just to wrong-foot ill-informed bluffers who imagine that Offenbach only wrote operettas.

The torch of operetta passed from Paris to Vienna in the 1870s and landed in the capable hands of the Waltz King **Johann Strauss the Younger (1825–99)**, whose *Die Fledermaus* (1874) has proved to have the most staying power of his 14 efforts in the genre. Inevitably, he also felt the need to write a conventional opera: *Ritter Pázmán,* which had its premiere on New Year's Day in 1892 and has never been heard of since.

After Strauss came the Hungarian **Franz Lehár (1870–1948)** and *The Merry Widow* (1905), one of a series of operettas that kept Vienna merrily waltzing up to and over the edge of disaster in 1914, with the help of others including Oscar Straus (note only one 's'), whose most famous work was *The Chocolate Soldier* (1908).

England, meanwhile, had developed its own very distinctive comic opera tradition through the collaboration of **W.S. Gilbert (1836–1911)** and **Arthur Sullivan (1842–1900)** who together produced 14 popular operettas between 1871 and 1896, including *HMS Pinafore* (1878), *The Pirates of Penzance* (1879), *Iolanthe* (1882) and *The Mikado* (1885). The bluffer should be aware that snobs like to look down on G&S, but Gilbert's wit and Sullivan's memorable tunes provide far better evenings of entertainment than many mainstays of the regular operatic canon.

Britain also embraced the Viennese works of Lehár and Straus with great enthusiasm, and did so again after the long, dark interval of 1914–18. The culmination of the operetta tradition was *The White Horse Inn* (1930) by **Ralph Benatzky (1884–1957)** and **Robert Stolz (1880–1975),** an extravaganza of gaily dancing Austrians that enjoyed huge success in London and New York. In this respect it may be considered a precursor to *The Sound of Music,* albeit with a much larger cast.

On the western side of the Atlantic, immigrant composers of operetta such as the Hungarian **Sigmund Romberg (1887–1951)** delighted audiences with the likes of *The Student Prince* (1924) and *The Desert Song* (1926). But by then the days of operetta as cutting-edge mass entertainment were drawing to a close, with the advent of the musical.

The singers in an operetta are much more likely to be classically trained in opera; those in musicals tend to be actors who can carry a tune.

THE MUSICAL

What is the difference between an operetta and a musical? The bluffer may confidently assert that both involve singing and talking, but that a musical tends to have a higher proportion of words and most likely involves dancing, too. The singers in an operetta are much more likely to be classically trained in opera; those in musicals tend to be actors who can carry a tune. But the line, as between opera and operetta, is a distinctly fuzzy one.

The first of the great American musicals, *Show Boat,* by **Jerome Kern (1885–1945)** and **Oscar Hammerstein II (1895–1960)** appeared in 1927 – the same year that saw the arrival of the talking picture in *The Jazz Singer,* itself a musical. Thereafter, great American exponents of the musical wrote for the movie studios as well as the stage. **Irving Berlin (1888–1989)** may have written comparatively little for the musical stage, but his movie credits include *Top Hat* (1935), *Holiday Inn* (1942) and *Easter Parade* (1948). **Cole Porter (1891–1964)** had a string of stage successes including *Paris* (1928), *Anything Goes* (1934) and *Kiss Me, Kate* (1948).

The bluffer may safely assert that the greatest American musical writer of the 20th century was **Richard Rodgers (1902–79)**, working first with the alcoholic lyricist **Lorenz Hart (1895–1943)** and then with Oscar Hammerstein II. The golden age of Rodgers and Hammerstein began with *Oklahoma!* in 1943 and continued through *Carousel* (1945), *South Pacific* (1949) and *The King and I* (1951) to *The Sound of Music* (1959), thanks in part to the masterful orchestrations by **Robert Russell Bennett (1894–1981)**. Like Gilbert and Sullivan before them, Rodgers and Hammerstein's work is prone to mockery by snobs but can actually afford as much spiritual uplift as the finest opera. Hence it comes as no surprise to find that *Carousel* and *South Pacific* have both been performed, in recent years, by mainstream opera companies.

Oscar Hammerstein II also penned the lyrics for the 1943 Broadway musical *Carmen Jones,* which uses Bizet's music but transforms the setting to an American parachute factory in the Second World War and uses an all-black cast. There can be few finer examples of blinkered prejudice than the conversation between two Edinburgh ladies overheard on leaving the city's Festival Theatre after a fine performance of *Carmen Jones* several years ago. After three hours of pure Bizet, one gestured to a poster advertising a forthcoming Scottish Opera season and suggested that they might give it a try. 'Och no,' replied her friend. 'Opera! I couldn't be doing with that nonsense!'

Other leading exponents of the American musical include **Leonard Bernstein (1918–1990)**, also a fine classical composer and conductor, whose best-known musicals include *On the Town* (1944) and *West Side Story* (1957). Both have been performed by opera companies, while *Candide* (1956) was written as an opera and subsequently revised as an operetta, and is regularly performed in opera houses around the world.

Similarly **Stephen Sondheim (1930–)** has already found his way into the operatic repertoire with *A Little Night Music* (1973) and *Sweeney Todd* (1979), while other works, including *Company* (1970), *Follies* (1971) and *Sunday in the Park with George* (1984), so far remain confined to the musical stage.

Britain's **Andrew Lloyd Webber (1948–)** is renowned for his operatic style of composition, featuring music throughout rather than with spoken dialogue in the manner of the Broadway musical. Other links with opera include the fact that his most successful show *The Phantom of the Opera* (1986 – and still running in London and New York in 2018) is (a) set in the Paris Opera House, and (b) features one tune so reminiscent of an *aria* from *La Fanciulla del West* that the Puccini estate was moved to sue him for plagiarism, a case that was settled out of court. So far *Phantom, Jesus Christ Superstar* (1970), *Evita* (1978), *Cats* (1981), *Starlight Express* (1984), *Aspects of Love* (1989), *Sunset Boulevard* (1993) and *The Woman in White* (2004) have yet to grace a single operatic stage… but give it time.

OPERA TODAY

While the public is voting with their wallets and purses for 32-year runs of *The Phantom of the Opera,* and opera companies are opening their programmes to Gilbert and Sullivan, Rodgers and Hammerstein, Bernstein, and Sondheim, others continue gamely composing conventional operas at the rate of 100 or so a year. The ideal modern opera justifies the large taxpayer subsidy that has financed its staging by containing few tunes, minimal action and playing to a half-empty house who will greet its conclusion with tumultuous applause to demonstrate how clever they are in seeing the Emperor fully clothed, perhaps mixed with a measure of relief.

Famed British contemporary opera composers include **Harrison Birtwistle (1934–)** whose best-known work is perhaps *Gawain* (1990), and **Peter Maxwell Davies (1934–2016)** whose chamber opera *The Lighthouse* (1979) breaks with tradition by telling a rather gripping tale.

Across the Atlantic, **Philip Glass (1937–)** dislikes the description of his music as 'minimalist' but is allegedly content with 'music with repetitive structures'. You can say that again. And again and again. To be fair, experience of *Akhnaten* (1984) and *The Making of the Representative for Planet 8* (1988) does confirm that Glass's music has a certain mesmeric quality. Though the true bluffer should await a performance of *Satyagraha* (1979), which is written in Sanskrit, and make a point of not needing to consult the surtitles.

Glass's fellow American **John Adams (1947–)** has most famously given the world *Nixon in China* (1987) and *The Death of Klinghoffer* (1991). It is known that someone who attended an early American performance of the latter has developed a means of rating every opera on his personal 'Klinghoffer scale', a measure of unenjoyability calibrated from 10 (*Klinghoffer*) to 0 (*The Marriage of Figaro*).

The next generation of British operatic composers has daringly departed from the mould by writing works that are actually enjoyable (though the bluffer should naturally try to keep this important information under his or her hat). Works that a respectable number of people would happily pay to see again include *Flight* (1998) by **Jonathan Dove (1959–)**, *The Silver Tassie* (2000) and *Anna Nicole* (2011) by **Mark-Anthony Turnage (1960–)** and *The Tempest* (2004) by **Thomas Adès (1971–)** which has already enjoyed two well-received runs at the Royal Opera House.

FOOTNOTE: WOMEN IN OPERA

Finally, the bluffer should be prepared to address the question of whether opera is an essentially misogynistic art, in which women are regularly portrayed as thick or mad and go on to die horrible deaths; and on which it is possible to write nine admittedly ill-informed chapters without mentioning a single female composer.

You should be aware of the existence of **Francesca Cazzini (1587–1641)** whose *La Liberazione di Ruggiero* (1625) is usually considered the first opera by a female composer. But after her there were three pretty blank centuries until British **Ethel Smyth (1858–1944)** whose most famous but regrettably still little performed work was *The Wreckers* (1906).

There are a number of female opera composers active today but few of their works make it to the stage, and it is sadly impossible to say whether this is due to centuries of disgracefully ingrained male prejudice or because they aren't much good. The bluffer should be able to get by with a knowledgeable mention of British **Judith Weir (1954–)**, appointed the first female Master of the Queen's Music in 2014, whose staged and critically acclaimed works include *A Night at the Chinese Opera* (1987) and *Blond Eckbert* (1994).

℔

There's no point in pretending that you know everything about opera – nobody does – but if you've got this far and you've absorbed at least a modicum of the information and advice contained within these pages, then you will almost certainly know more than 99% of the rest of the human race about what opera is, who performs it, who watches it, why, and where. What you now do with this information is up to you, but here's a suggestion: be confident about your new-found knowledge, see how far it takes you, but above all have fun using it. You are now a bona fide expert in the art of bluffing about the world's most arcane and enigmatic musical art form.

CURTAIN CALL: A USEFUL GLOSSARY

Operatic term	Official meaning	Real meaning
Allegro con brio	(of music) fast with enthusiasm.	Disappointing 1970s British motor car, surprisingly converted to run on soft cheese.
Alto	Countertenor (q.v.).	Stop right there.
Aria	Air (musical, not the sort you breathe).	The bit with a tune.
Arpeggio	Musical technique of playing the notes of a chord one after the other, not together.	Plays right back for Manchester City.
Baritone	Male singer too low to be a tenor but not low enough to be a bass.	Hereditary honour for English cathedral choirmasters, ranking just below a baronet.

Operatic term	Official meaning	Real meaning
Baron Ochs	Buffoonish suitor of Sophie in *Der Rosenkavalier*.	Slightly kinder description of a *castrato* (q.v.).
Bass	Male singer with lowest vocal range.	British ale traditionally popular with male singers.
Bel canto	Beautiful singing.	An art practised in the 18th and 19th centuries, now long forgotten.
Castrato	Male *soprano*, castrated before puberty: not made illegal in Italy until 1870.	Two suggestive scoops of Neapolitan ice cream.
Chorus	Supporting cast of singers.	Those denied a decent role in the production on the grounds of inexperience, ugliness or alcoholism.
Coloratura	Musical ornamentation.	Using more notes than the composer could be bothered to write.
Contralto	The deepest female singing voice, very rarely encountered in practice.	Extinct species of bird; see also 'dodo'.

Operatic term	Official meaning	Real meaning
Countertenor	Male *soprano*, *mezzo-soprano* or contralto.	Soft-hearted modern replacement for the *castrato*, relying on tight underwear rather than a sharp knife.
Crush bar	Legendary Covent Garden former watering hole, now a restaurant.	Bar serving only non-alcoholic fruit juices; a safe bet if seeking to avoid musicians.
Diva	Celebrated female singer.	One of the more enterprising *Pearl Fishers*.
Farinelli	The most famous Italian *castrato*.	Pasta, traditionally served with two meatballs.
Gio Compario	Ludicrous parody of the traditional fat, operatic tenor, used to advertise the Gocompare.com price comparison website.	What the average ITV viewer expects to find in an opera house, justifying his decision never to go to one.
Gluck	18th-century composer.	The disappointing sound made by a champagne bottle at your Glyndebourne picnic when it stops going 'glug'.

Operatic term	Official meaning	Real meaning
High C	Classic operatic high note, two octaves above Middle C.	Where the *Titanic* sank.
Intermezzo	Comic interlude in *opera seria* (q.v.).	Person who fancies *sopranos* wearing trousers.
La Donna è Mobile	The woman is fickle.	A request to hand over your smartphone.
Long interval	Break in the performance in which one may dine as well as drink.	The one bit of country-house opera everyone enjoys.
Marschallin	Unfaithful wife of a field marshal in *Der Rosenkavalier*.	Crowd control at Bayreuth.
Mezzo-soprano	Halfway between a *soprano* and a *contralto*.	Neither one thing nor the other.
Opera buffa	Comic opera.	Nude opera (sadly rarely performed since the demise of David Freeman's Opera Factory in 1998).

Operatic term	Official meaning	Real meaning
Opera seria	Serious opera.	Opera that goes on a bit, so that you feel that you are actually watching a series.
Operetta	Light opera.	Opera sponsored by the English Table Tennis Association (ETTA).
O Welche Lust	The prisoners' chorus from Fidelio.	Something unspeakable in the valleys of west Wales, involving sheep.
Pit	Place where the orchestra sits.	Dirty and dangerous English workplace, thoughtfully closed down by Mrs Thatcher.
Prima donna	First lady; principal *soprano*.	Any very difficult and demanding member of an opera company, i.e., pretty much all of them (male or female).
Recitative	Sung speech between arias.	The bits of the libretto for which the composer could not be bothered to write a tune.
Soprano	Higher female singing voice.	American mobster.

Operatic term	Official meaning	Real meaning
Tenor	Male singing voice above baritone and below *soprano*.	Operatic character who will probably beat the baritone and end up on top of the *soprano*.
The Ring	Wagner's four-opera masterpiece.	Rubber device required to sit through Wagner's four-opera masterpiece.
Theorbo	Large stringed instrument in baroque orchestras, aka chitarrone or archlute.	One of the many things you should never offer to transport on your bicycle.
Tito Gobbi	Celebrated Italian baritone.	Peridontal disease most common in the former Yugloslavia.
Wally	Heroine of Catalani's eponymous opera.	Apt description of anyone who throws themselves into an avalanche.